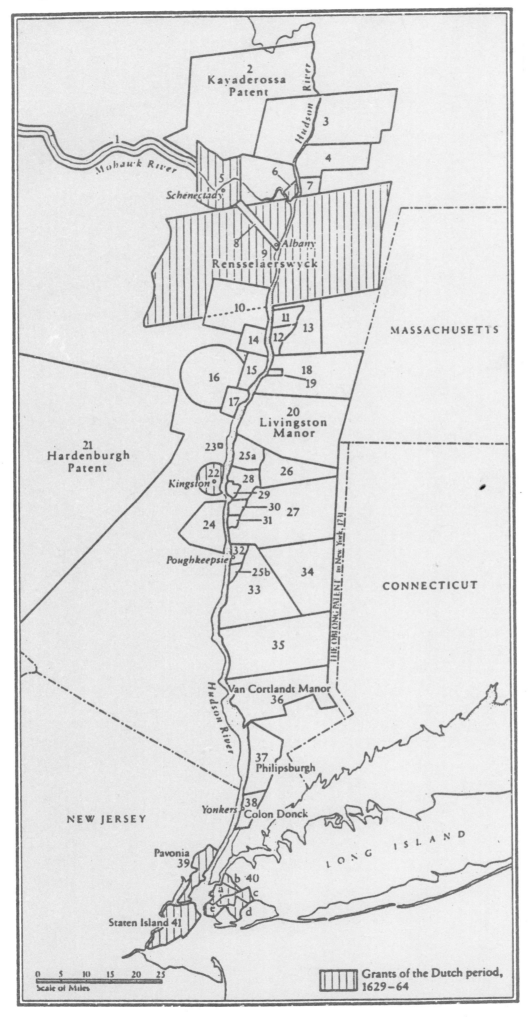

2
Kayaderossa
Patent

3

1

Mohawk River

4

5
Schenectady

6

7

8

9 Albany
Rensselaerswyck

10

11

13

MASSACHUSETTS

14

12

15

16

18

19

17

20
Livingston
Manor

21
Hardenburgh
Patent

23

25a

26

22
Kingston

28

29

30

27

24

31

32
Poughkeepsie

25b

34

CONNECTICUT

33

35

Van Cortlandt Manor
36

Hudson River

37
Philipsburgh

Yonkers
38
Colon Donck

NEW JERSEY

Pavonia
39

b 40
a
c
e d

Staten Island 41

LONG ISLAND

THE ORIGINAL PATENT in New York, 1714

0 5 10 15 20 25
Scale of Miles

Grants of the Dutch period,
1629–64

Great Houses *of the* Hudson River

Great Houses
of the

Hudson River

Edited by Michael Middleton Dwyer

Preface by Mark F. Rockefeller

Aerial Photography by Steve Turner

Published in association with
Historic Hudson Valley

A Bulfinch Press Book
Little, Brown and Company
Boston • New York • London

A Charles Davey *design* production
945 West End Avenue, New York, NY 10025

First Edition

ISBN 0-8212-2767-X

Library of Congress Control Number 2001089095

ACKNOWLEDGEMENTS

Those "...little, nameless, unremembered acts/ of kindness..."wrote Wordsworth walking
back from a re-visit to Tintern Abbey, a beautiful Cistercian abbey, now in ruins, on the banks
of the River Wye in Wales. While the houses in this book are far from ruins, Wordsworth's
lines echoed in my mind as, driving back to New York, I contemplated the impossible task of
writing these acknowledgements which can do little justice to all those who have helped in
the making of this book. You may have forgotten your acts of kindness: I have not.
This book is a Charles Davey design concept, in association with Historic Hudson Valley. For
four years, McKelden Smith has made HHV a home to me, and to him goes my utter gratitude
for all his help and advice. To Waddell Stillman who backed me and my idea, and all the staff
at Historic Hudson Valley who have been a part of this project. To Mark Rockefeller for his
Preface; to Bill Lickle, who introduced me to HHV, and to Michael Sand at Bulfinch, who
believed me enough to publish the book. To Bruce Naramore, who vetted the first list of
houses, and advised me as to its merit; and to Catha Grace Rambush, whose text was the first I
received and who supported me as the book took shape. Many people contributed drafts for
the text and captions. We are not attributing names as the editing was done with a view to
giving the book one voice. I am indebted to those who did give of their time, advice or
research. Among these were: Marcy Shaffer, Judy Harris, Sharon Palmer, Roderic Blackburn,
Linda McLean, Evelyn Trebilcock, Bruce Naramore, Susan Howard, Ginger Shore, Diane
Rosasco, Marvin Swartz, Melodye Moore, John Sears, Ann Jordan, Diane Boyce, Alan Daly,
Frank Futral, Denise van Buren, Ray Armiter, Kenneth Snodgrass, Charles Lyle, Cynthia
Altman, Laura Vookles, Zoe Lindsay, Alix Schnee, Charles Casimiro, Linda and Duane
Watson, Virginia Hancock, Mary Flad, and Diane Botnick.
Specific photo credits are at the back of this book, but my gratitude to everyone who has
helped turn ideas into images with their photography, notably Steve Turner, Mick Hales, Ted
Spiegel, and Bill Urbin. Others who helped with permissions or research are Angela Giral,
Cheryl Gold, Al Moskowitz, Burns Patterson, Dennis Wentworth, and the staffs at the New
York State Office of Parks, Recreation and Historic Preservation and the National Park Service.
This book would not have been possible without the generous help of The Franklin & Eleanor
Roosevelt Institute and the incisive intervention of David Woolner, its Executive Director.

Bulfinch Press is an imprint and trademark of Little, Brown and Company (Inc.).

Printed in Italy by Cover Communications

Contents

Preface

Along with everyone in my family, I have always loved the Hudson Valley and its history. And the great houses of the Hudson River tell an important and fascinating part of the story. I was lucky enough to have spent my childhood living in one of them. But I think I would still have a passionate interest in Hudson Valley history without that privilege. The history of this place is so

"Early Twilight, Kaatskill Landing and Mountains from the East Bank of the Hudson River, NY," by George Harvey. The river, and the mountains, were at the center of America's psychological and physical development in the 19th century, and the Hudson River was a cradle for America's artists and the development of its culture. Collection of Historic Hudson Valley.

rich, so broad, so deep, and so consistently profound that it would have been impossible for me to have escaped its beneficent influence. I admit my enthusiasm for these great landmarks without hesitation or apology.

Simply as documents, these houses represent an amazing range of accomplishment and endeavor. Where else can you find the home of a president like Franklin D. Roosevelt, a humanitarian like Eleanor Roosevelt, an artist like Frederic Church, a writer like Washington Irving, an inventor like Samuel F.B. Morse, and—if you will permit me—an entrepreneur and philanthropist like John D. Rockefeller? Where else can you find the architecture of

Alexander Jackson Davis, Calvert Vaux, Stanford White, and Charles F. McKim, the landscapes and gardens of Andrew Jackson Downing, Charles Platt, and André Parmentier? Whatever your interest in history—whether it be politics, the military, art, architecture, science, business, the decorative arts, social history, agriculture, or practically anything else—you will find someone here who played an essential role on a national scale and some place here that can bring it to life for you when you make a visit.

When you visit these houses, you will see their interiors and their contents, of particular interest to antiquarians and specialists. What I marvel at, however, is that at so many places, the contents have remained in place and depict the past with such riveting authenticity. At Montgomery Place, for example, nothing was apparently ever thrown away, so you can soak up the spirit of the past two hundred years. If Franklin and Eleanor Roosevelt returned to Springwood, or if Washington Irving returned to Sunnyside, or if Frederick Vanderbilt returned to Hyde Park, or if Frederic Church returned to Olana, they would see virtually nothing changed. And so you have the very personal experience of seeing these places through their eyes.

As you read this book, you will learn about the architects, the owners and builders, the successive generations of tenants, and the facts of the history of these houses. I encourage you to go further, however, and make plans to visit these places. When you get there, you will hear their stories. Listen first to the script of the tour guide. Then pause and listen to the secrets whispered quietly through the haze of memory. You will hear stories of daily life from times gone by—how people were born, how they died, how they cooked and served their food, how they ate and drank. You will learn how they grew up and married, how they raised their children, what kind of human relationships were formed around their lives. The stories will charm you and touch your heart, they will make you laugh, they will make you cry, they will inspire you and make you proud. Some will even make you angry. Everywhere you will hear stories that will arouse your curiosity and send you in a bee-line to the library (or the Internet) to discover more.

As is apparent from the table of contents, not every house of consequence is included—in fact, far from it. Along the river are many more houses, mostly in private hands, which are being lived in by families like yours, or which have been adapted for use for other purposes. And between all of these houses are towns, villages, hamlets, and simple cross-roads filled with vernacular buildings of interest and distinction, and farmland, parkland, and valuable open space, all of which are essential to the Hudson Valley's sense of place.

This guidebook is your invitation to explore the great domestic landmarks of the Hudson Valley and the communities where they can be found. I hope you will make this book a checklist of places to explore and get to know more fully.

I particularly hope that this book will inspire you to join the cause of historic preservation if you have not done so already. Despite the tranquil domesticity apparently enjoyed by most of these impressive houses, they are all threatened in various ways.

Leaky roofs, peeling paint, invasive weeds, rot, and other problems familiar to homeowners everywhere are continuously worrisome. Even more serious is the threat of sprawling, unchecked growth of towns and cities, the destruction of farms, and the ugliness that can creep into the urban and rural landscape, spoiling the context of these great landmarks. You can help by lending your voice to the growing chorus demanding smart growth policies everywhere.

You can help by joining a friends group or a preservation organization like Historic Hudson Valley or the National Trust for Historic Preservation, or the Friends of Clermont, or the Friends of the Mills Mansion, or the Olana Partnership, for example. You can join your local historical society, preservation group, or conservation advocate. Every gift of time, money, and interest—large or small—makes a difference.

As you read through this book and visit these places, I believe you will agree with me that your efforts will be extraordinarily well-justified.

Mark F. Rockefeller
Chairman, Historic Hudson Valley
Pocantico Hills, New York

ABOVE The porter's lodge, Springside, Poughkeepsie, New York, sporting a new roof and painted in its original colors as selected by Andrew Jackson Downing in 1850.

Springside is the only surviving domestic landscape design by Downing. In 1969 it was designated a National Historic Landscape primarily because of its association with Downing. Tragically, that year a fire destroyed the carriage house and stables; the main house had previously collapsed, leaving only the porter's lodge remaining of the buildings, together with Downing's extraordinary landscaping. It survives now due to the efforts of a handful of local people who, together with two environmental groups, Hudson River Heritage and Clearwater, first sued to preserve the historic portion of the site and then in 1986 helped form a nonprofit group, Springside Landscape Restoration. After intense work including the commissioning of a site analysis in 1989, published as Springside National Historic Landmark Master Plan, *in 1990 Springside Landscape Restoration finally took ownership of the historic portion of the site, just under twenty acres.*

Springside was the result of a remarkable collaboration between noted philanthropist Matthew Vassar and the renowned architect Andrew Jackson Downing. In the 1850s, Vassar, a successful businessman (who also founded Vassar College), together with the Poughkeepsie village council, determined to create a rural cemetery, an idea then much in vogue. Vassar purchased the land on his own account, and enlisted the support of Downing, who lived in nearby Newburgh. Together they developed the site to be "compatible for either a rural cemetery or a country estate." The cemetery never gained the needed subscribers, and in 1851 Vassar began construction of his private estate. Tragically, Downing was killed the following year, before Springside was completed. The extent of his design for its landscape is uncertain and there are no known plans although several plans exist for the buildings. The site was completed, however, and Vassar moved in in 1864; he died in 1868.

Throughout much of the 19th and 20th centuries Springside was part of a neighborhood of country estates extending from Poughkeepsie to Wappinger Falls, including Locust Grove, Maple Grove, and Springside. Like Springside, Maple Grove (below) is also undergoing restoration. In 2001 it was added to the National Register of Historic Places and a Historic Structure Report has just been completed as the basis for future restoration.
BELOW The façade of Maple Grove.

Introduction

Along the east bank of the Hudson River, from Albany to New York, stands as important a group of houses as anywhere in America. This book is your invitation to explore them. The Hudson Valley was, in the 18th century, American history's center stage, and in the mid-19th century men like A.J. Davis, A.J. Downing, and the painters of the Hudson River School made it America's cultural epicenter. Even without these associations, the overpowering natural beauty of the valley and its extraordinary scenic aspects were ready-made for houses, gardens, and landscape parks of great distinction.

Detail from a 1730 map of the northern colonies, with an inset view of early Manhattan and its Dutch-style architecture. The engraving shows enslaved Africans bearing New World riches to the King of England.
Collection of Historic Hudson Valley.

For centuries before the arrival of the Dutch, the Wekquaesgeeks, Sint Sinks, Mahikans, and others farmed, hunted, and fished on the banks of the river explored in 1609 by Henry Hudson. At first, the Native Americans and Europeans were content trading furs and other valuable commodities, but soon the Europeans decided to acquire land. The clash of values, the cultural differences regarding the concept of land ownership, disease, and war eventually drove away the region's remaining original inhabitants.

New Netherland, as the first European settlement was known, became the English colony of New York in 1664.

Tracts of land, some enormous, were bought from the Native Americans and Europeans by men with capital, often for investment. Crown patents were issued for these as confirmation of title. Land on manors was typically developed by tenant farmers who held long-term leases.

By the beginning of the 18th century, much of the land along the east side of the Hudson River was held in the form of large manorial grants or as freeholds (see endpaper map). Philipsburg Manor, for example, consisted of 52,000 acres; Van Cortlandt Manor 86,000 acres, and Livingston Manor 160,000 acres.

The earliest houses, such as the Van Alen House, reflected the medieval building traditions of the Dutch, Germans, French Huguenots, and other northern Europeans who settled here. They built with stone, wood, and locally made brick, combined with materials imported from Europe. After 1664, the English influence began to alter northern European building traditions, especially in New York City. In the upper reaches of the river, however, established customs prevailed well into the 18th century. A few houses with fine Georgian detail were built before the Revolution, such as Schuyler Mansion in Albany and Philipse Manor Hall in Yonkers, but these were the exceptions to the rule.

The 17th and 18th century manorial system of land ownership allowed 19th century estate builders to acquire large amounts of acreage along the Hudson. Particularly along the east side of the river, houses were built that were much more elaborate than those that came before. Some were built by the descendants of large landholders, such as the children of Robert and Margaret Beekman Livingston, who built a series of substantial houses between Tivoli and Staatsburg. Others were built by the local gentry, such as Peter Van Ness, a lawyer in Kinderhook, who built Lindenwald, and his brother, David Van Ness, a merchant in Red Hook, who built the nearly identical Maizefield. Still others were built by affluent New Yorkers, such as States Dyckman at Boscobel, who hoped to live as country gentlemen and to escape the crowding and periodic epidemics of New York City.

There was a remarkable uniformity to the houses built

after the Revolution, especially among those built upriver. Influenced by English Georgian architecture, house-builders used masonry to build rectangular, two story structures, with symmetrically placed windows and decorative elements. There were usually four rooms and fireplaces on the main floor, organized around a central hall and staircase. The rooms were gracious and generously proportioned, with high ceilings, finely detailed mantelpieces, and plaster cornices. The Hudson River was lined with houses from the Federal period, once plentiful but now rare. Some were destroyed, and many, such as Montgomery Place and Lindenwald, were altered in the 19th century.

This is a rare 18th-century panoramic scene. It shows the confluence of the Nepperhan and Hudson rivers, where Philipse Manor was built. One can clearly see the strategic placing of the manor in this commanding position. Collection of Historic Hudson Valley.

After the Erie Canal opened in 1825, New York City became the nation's commercial center and largest port. As the city grew, so did the desire on the part of its wealthiest inhabitants to build villas in the countryside, to which they could escape occasionally or spend their retirement. It was only natural that as New York grew wealthy the arts flourished. In the 1820s and 1830s, New York fell under the sway of romanticism, as exemplified in part by the writing of Washington Irving, James Fenimore Cooper, and other authors who set many of their tales in the region.

The most influential of these writers was Washington Irving. In 1835, Irving purchased an 18th century farmhouse in Tarrytown, on land once part of Philipsburg Manor, and transformed it into his image of a Dutch colonial cottage. Adding stepped gables, columned chimney stacks, weather vanes, irregular windows, and other details including, most amusingly, the false date of 1656, Irving created a fictionalized, romantic cottage meant to recall sentimentally the early architectural history of the colony. Irving, along with his romantic contemporaries, advocated the idea of landscape and building interacting on one palette. Irving designed his own pastoral natural landscape and even planted wisteria vines (unbelievably, still growing) which climbed the walls and enveloped the house.

Alexander Jackson Davis, born in New York City in 1803, was one of the most original and inventive architects practicing in pre-Civil War America. His work helped shape the American aesthetic of the time. Davis's architectural practice was wide-ranging, but his identity as a taste-maker lies in the Hudson Valley. Today, visitors can see two great Davis masterpieces illustrating his versatility—Lyndhurst, the greatest Gothic Revival house in America, and Montgomery Place, designed in a lush Classical Revival style. Davis saw the Gothic and the Classical not as opposites but as complementary parts of the Romantic. He had several dozen Hudson Valley commissions, including the Italianate villa Locust Grove, and the Gothic library at Edgewater.

Davis's collaboration with Andrew Jackson Downing in the Hudson Valley was a remarkable happenstance, for, if Davis was one of the greatest and most important architects of the 19th century in America, Downing was one of the greatest and most important "landscape gardeners." Together these two idealists determined the course of domestic architecture in America for two generations. Downing was a native of Newburgh, New York, and lived in the region most of his short life. Nonetheless, his reputation, earned largely through his critical writing, was international and had far-reaching effects. Through his publishing, his designs and design philosophy were exported from the Hudson Valley to the rest of the nation.

Architecture and landscape gardening styles more or less invented in the Hudson Valley had broad national impact, to be sure, but the Hudson River School of painting is even better known today. The great painters of the Hudson River School lived and worked to varying degrees in New York and the Hudson Valley. Among them were Thomas Cole, Asher B. Durand, Albert Bierstadt, Jasper Cropsey, and Frederic Church. The Thomas Cole house survives, though barely, but Frederic Church's country house, Olana, is preserved and offers astonishing insights into the man and his work. The house is both a three-dimensional painting of the Hudson River School, and, like Washington Irving's Sunnyside, an autobiography of the artist himself.

In the 1890s, the inevitable reaction against romanticism set in, and the villas of A. J. Davis and Richard Upjohn and the paintings of the Hudson River School came to look old-fashioned. The World's Columbian Exposition of 1892-93, with its brilliant white Classical architecture, signaled the end of the picturesque styles and heralded a revival of Classicism, often called the Beaux-Arts or American Renaissance style. For many, the new architecture was a revival of American Colonial design. But for the very rich,

"View from Montgomery Place," A.J. Davis. The sketch illustrates Downing's and Davis's concern for a smooth transition from the interior of the house to the surrounding countryside. Collection of Avery Library, Columbia University.

New York's architectural establishment, led by Richard Morris Hunt and McKim, Mead & White, designed a series of extravagant houses that found their inspiration in the palaces of Europe. While other places such as Newport, Rhode Island, for example, are more famous for their Gilded Age ostentation, some houses of this type were built in the Hudson River Valley. The Staatsburgh estate was built for Ogden Mills, who provided the money, and his wife, Ruth Livingston, who provided heritage and social status. They hired Stanford White to transform a Greek Revival house into a curious stage-set backdrop for Mrs. Mills, who was an ambitious society hostess. Just up the road, the Frederick Vanderbilts hired McKim, Mead, and White and completed a limestone mansion in 1898 that would have been perfectly at home in Newport.

Shortly thereafter, Franklin Roosevelt and his mother put a new Colonial Revival front onto their mid-19th century Italianate villa. Like Staatsburgh, it, too, became a kind of stage set, not for social positioning, but for Franklin Roosevelt's brilliant political career. Both Franklin and Eleanor found the need to retreat even from Springwood. Eleanor needed to retreat from her overbearing mother-in-law and built Val-Kill for herself and her friends. The house, though architecturally unremarkable, resonates because Eleanor, arguably, was the most important—and controversial—woman in American history. Top Cottage, which Franklin largely designed himself in a vernacular Hudson Valley style, was among the first houses in America built for wheelchair accessibility.

About the time that the Roosevelts were expanding Springwood, the great entrepreneur John D. Rockefeller, whose creation of Standard Oil changed the course of international business history, made his first purchases of land in Westchester County and moved into a rambling frame house. When it burned in 1902, he and his son John D. Rockefeller, Jr. undertook the construction of the last great Hudson Valley villa to be built. The Beaux-Arts-style house and its expansive gardens, completed in 1913, took full advantage of the breathtaking site. William Welles Bosworth, an architect at the beginning of his career, fully understood and developed the site's landscape design potential.

The era of great house building was brought to a halt by the Great Depression. The modern movement in architecture, with its emphasis on the expression of function and structure, produced some notable work in the Hudson Valley. Only Manitoga, however, built in 1951 for the designer Russell Wright, is open to the public.

Efforts to preserve the architectural legacy of the Hudson Valley have deep roots. Among the earliest was the gift of Philipse Manor Hall to the state of New York in 1908. In 1922, the city of Yonkers purchased the Glenview Mansion, then just forty-five years old, to preserve it as a park and museum. In 1938, during the Depression, the state government accepted Staatsburgh as a gift from Gladys Mills Phipps.

The federal government first assumed responsibility for the preservation of the Vanderbilt Mansion in 1940, accepting the property as a gift under pressure from President Franklin Roosevelt, who appreciated it more for the historic landscape created by André Parmentier than for its grand architecture. Roosevelt left his own home, Springwood, to the National Park Service. Regrettably, however, preservation in Hyde Park did not extend to its village setting, and the town was spoiled by development so remarkably insensitive that it was the subject of a public television documentary.

Historic preservation efforts in the Hudson Valley began in a more formal way by John D. Rockefeller, Jr., who had financed the painstaking preservation program at Williamsburg. His involvement at Philipsburg Manor began in 1940. In 1945 Rockefeller purchased Sunnyside, and by doing so broke new ground. Prior to that, most preservation efforts were concentrated on landmarks of the colonial and federal eras and on landmarks associated with political and military heroes. By contrast, Sunnyside was a mid-19th century landmark associated with a literary figure who had been dead for only eighty-five years. The two properties became the core of Sleepy Hollow Restorations, a private foundation he started in 1951. In 1953 John D. Rockefeller, Jr., made his first purchases of land and buildings at Van Cortlandt Manor, adding them to the Sleepy Hollow Restorations network. In the 1980s, this foundation became

Historic Hudson Valley, incorporating Montgomery Place and the Union Church of Pocantico Hills.

In the 1970s, the decade of the Bicentennial, the Park Service renewed its commitment in the Hudson Valley to acquire properties with historical association. In 1974, the National Park Service acquired Lindenwald, the Van Buren house. In 1977 Eleanor Roosevelt's Val-Kill was added to the roster, and in 2001 the National Park Service assumed responsibility for Top Cottage and opened it to the public, forming an integrated complex of buildings and sites that tell the story of Franklin and Eleanor Roosevelt. In 2000, Scenic Hudson stepped in to preserve open space in the vicinity of the Roosevelt estate, not a minute too soon.

New York State Office of Parks, Recreation, and Historic Preservation has continued building its own collection of historic places in its Taconic Region. In 1962, the state added Clermont, a combination gift and sale from Livingston heirs. Olana was rescued by private citizens with public money, the state taking title in 1966. Both Olana and Clermont, in addition to Staatsburgh, were acquired as much for their outstanding parkland as for their architecture and history, an approach that anticipated by a generation the current thinking of preservationists about the relationship between land and buildings.

The National Trust for Historic Preservation began its role in the Hudson Valley in 1961, when it received Lyndhurst by bequest. This assured the long term survival of this great American house, complete with its furnishings, grounds, and outbuildings. Gov. Nelson A. Rockefeller left his share of Kykuit, the Rockefeller family's great Hudson River villa, to the National Trust when he died in 1979. With the financial support of Governor Rockefeller's surviving brothers, Laurance S. and David Rockefeller, and the Rockefeller Brothers Fund, Kykuit was opened to the public, and the house, its magnificent gardens, and Governor Rockefeller's extraordinary 20th century sculpture collection were preserved intact. Historic Hudson Valley, founded in 1951 as Sleepy Hollow Restorations by John D. Rockefeller, Jr., opened the estate to the public in 1994 and operates public programs at Kykuit.

Strenuous efforts have been made by numerous other organizations and individuals who have taken on individual houses as labors of love, in many cases struggling against daunting odds. In Poughkeepsie, a private organization has assured a future for A.J. Davis's Locust Grove, which opened to the public in 1979. Preservation of Wilderstein, a spectacular Queen Anne style landmark built for the wonderfully eccentric Suckley family and set in a landscape by Calvert Vaux, has since 1980 been undertaken by a dedicat-

"A Morning Rainbow," attributed to George Harvey. A highly romantic view of Blithewood, showing the integration of the landscape into the design of the great estates of the Hudson River. Collection of Historic Hudson Valley.

ed group of preservationists who are bringing the house back bit by bit. And in Yonkers, the Hudson River Museum has recently restored some of the Glenview Mansion's Gilded Age interiors to great effect. Other examples of successful private efforts can be found in the pages of this book.

Today the emphasis is shifting to address the issue of context. Preservationists are insisting that the larger-scale environment of historic landmarks be preserved, in addition to the landmarks themselves, as sprawl and insensitive development have become even bigger preservation issues than peeling paint or leaking roofs. The modern environmental movement was born in the Hudson Valley when Scenic Hudson successfully sued to stop the development of Storm King Mountain into a pump storage facility in a 17-year long legal battle beginning in 1963. Scenic Hudson, the Open Space Institute, Hudson Valley Heritage, and other organizations have encouraged the preservation of open space, scenic "viewsheds," and other aspects of the Hudson River aesthetic. Scenic Hudson alone has preserved over 15,000 acres of threatened Hudson Valley landscape.

In 1996, the federal government designated the Hudson Valley as a National Heritage Area, and, in 1998, designated the Hudson River as a Heritage River. In partnership with the Greenway Communities Council and Greenway Conservancy, the State of New York, and numerous private organizations, the National Park Service has initiated the long-term process to provide comprehensive heritage and conservation planning, beginning a hopeful new era for historic preservation and heritage tourism in the Hudson Valley.

Kathleen Eagen Johnson
McKelden Smith
Historic Hudson Valley

Schuyler Mansion

In 1630, Kiliaen Van Rensselaer, one of the original directors of the Dutch West India Company, established the colony of Rensselaerswyck, comprising the existing counties of Albany and Rensselaer. Fort Orange had been built several years earlier, and in the shadow of this fort, Van Rensselaer's colonists built a number of crude wood-frame houses. In 1652, Peter Stuyvesant, the Director of New Netherland, laid out a new village called Beverwyck, later known as Albany, a village of freeholds that was distinct and separate from the surrounding colony of Rensselaerswyck. The houses built in the village were typically two-and-one-half stories tall, with steeply pitched roofs, brick walls, and the stepped parapets so characteristic of the Dutch style of house building. In 1664, the English took over the administration of New Netherland. It is an indication of the insularity of the residents of Albany, as well as the strength of their traditions, that another century passed before the Dutch style gave way to that of the English.

The first and most notable example of the new fashion was Schuyler Mansion, the house of Philip Schuyler, built in 1761 about one-half mile south of the stockaded city. It followed by six years or so the Georgian-style alterations of Frederick Philipse III at the Philipse Manor Hall in Yonkers and was a radical departure from the existing architecture of Albany. One visitor in 1765 called Albany a "dull and ill built" town but added that "One Mr. P. Schuyler has a good house…lately built in a better Stile, than I have generally seen in America."

ABOVE *A portrait of Philip and Catherine's son, Philip Jeremiah Schuyler, overlooks the mahogany dropleaf table set with a reproduction Wedgewood-style creamware. The feather pattern of the place settings recreates the daily plateware used by the Schuylers as documented by archaeological finds on the grounds. Beneath the Chippendale-style gold leaf mirror sits a circa 1800 sideboard attributed to the Massachusetts shop of John and Thomas Seymour. A 1792 silver epergne atop a mirrored plateau would have been used to serve fruits and nuts for dessert. The door visible in the right-hand corner led to the now demolished outbuildings. A working courtyard once included the kitchen, nursery, chicken coop, laundry, woodshed, privy, and office for General Schuyler.*

Schuyler was born in Albany in 1733. He was the grandnephew of Albany's first mayor, Pieter Schuyler. His family was rich and prominent and connected by marriage to a number of the Hudson Valley's great established families, including the Livingstons and the Van Cortlandts. Schuyler himself married Catherine Van Rensselaer in 1755. He served as a commissioned officer in the French and Indian Wars and committed himself to the side of the American colonies both before and during the American Revolution. He represented New York at the Continental Congress in Philadelphia and was best known for his role as Major General under George Washington. After the war, he was elected to the New York State Senate, the United States Senate, and ran twice for Governor of New York. As a businessman he amassed a fortune through his timber mills and herring fishery and exported the products from these businesses to as far away as Jamaica and Antigua. His elegant house on the hill, built when he was only twenty-eight years old, proclaimed to one and all his wealth, good taste, and social position.

ABOVE *The family parlor, or sitting room, restored to its 1790s appearance, is decorated with a flocked wallpaper similar to that purchased by Schuyler in England, and following an extensive paint analysis, the walls are painted in a vibrant yellow matched to samples of the original paint. The open Bible on the corner table was an heirloom from Schuyler's Dutch ancestors and dates to 1719. Important Schuyler family dates, such as births and marriages, are handwritten into the bible's endpages. The Chippendale chairs and sofa have been reupholstered in a reproduction silk damask to match the fabric purchased by Schuyler in England in 1761.*

ABOVE *The best parlor, situated in the desirable southeast corner of the house overlooked the Schuylers' formal gardens to the south and the Hudson River to the east. Schuyler purchased a "neat Mache ceiling" to adorn this room while in England in 1761-62. The Hepplewhite shieldback chairs, dated between 1790-1800, part of a set of eight, became popular following the 1788 publication of George Hepplewhite's* Cabinetmaker and Upholsterer's Guide. *The tall mahogany case clock with broken-arch pediment bonnet and three brass urn finials is the work of Schenectady cabinetmaker Jeremiah Knowles and Schenectady clockmaker Eliphalet Hull. A mahogany Hepplewhite-style pianoforte is visible beneath the full-length portrait of Alexander Hamilton and is a typical piece found in upper-class homes such as the Schuylers'. It is in this room that the wedding of the Schuyler's daughter, Elizabeth, to Alexander Hamilton took place in December 1780.*

While the house was being built, Schuyler traveled to England to tend to the military finances of his mentor, Colonel John Bradstreet. In return, Bradstreet looked after the construction of Schuyler's house. The Marquis de Chastellux described Schuyler as the house's "owner as well as its architect," but four craftsmen are known to be responsible for its execution: William Waldron, master mason; Lucas Hooghkerk, master brickmaker; John Gaborial and John Brown, carpenters. With the exception of a vestibule added around 1815 by a subsequent owner, the exterior of the house looks much as it did in 1761.

RIGHT Schuyler's first floor library held over 200 volumes of books on history, philosophy, religion, government, business, and mathematics—some pages of his mathematical calculations still exist. Having received little formal education, Schuyler was nevertheless a learned man and in an age when the average person was illiterate, Schuyler's collection of books was extraordinary. His prestigious social position demanded that he keep up with considerable

LEFT *The upstairs hall, called a "salon" or "saloon" (both meaning gathering place) may have been used for dancing the minuet, the ragamundo, and the allemondo, popular dances during the 18th century. During the summer this would have been an airy and comfortable room and may be the hall that Schuyler referred to in a letter describing his grandson learning to walk "toddling up and down the hall." His youngest daughter, Catherine, also most likely received her dance lessons here. Markings on the four Queen Anne chairs on the left, indicate that they were part of a much larger set, possibly as many as 14-16 chairs. They are believed to be part of the original furnishings of Schuyler Mansion. Without a fireplace or any means of heat, this area was probably little used in wintertime. The panoramic block-printed wallpaper, "El Dorado," was installed by New York State in 1915 at the time of the original restoration prior to the house opening as a historical museum. Designed in 1848 by Eugene Ehrmann, Joseph Fuchs, and Georges Zipelius, and first printed in 1849, it continues to be manufactured by the Zuber Wallpaper firm in France. It depicts views of scenes in Mexico, Europe, Asia, and Africa. In 1761 Schuyler purchased an English paper, "Ruins of Rome," as depicted by scenes designed to simulate framed oil paintings. Ten "paintings" were shipped back to Albany and are believed to have been installed in the halls on the first and second floors of the mansion.*

amounts of correspondence, and of course he had to keep the affairs of his estate and businesses in order. His grandson once wrote that he began his work here at 5:00 in the morning and did not rest until noontime. The Chippendale corner chair, also known as a roundabout chair, is most commonly found in New York. Its design is typically male as its user would have needed to straddle the seat, prohibiting a woman from maintaining a ladylike posture.

ABOVE *Originally decorated with scenic "Ruins of Rome" wallpaper, the large entrance hall now features a portrait of Philip Schuyler, a copy of a miniature by John Trumbull. The elaborate staircase features three balusters per stair, each with a different type of spiral turning, designed by an unknown craftsman.*

Schuyler, the man of business and military affairs, directed his talents while abroad to the decoration of his new house. He was surely impressed by the sophisticated architecture of mid-century London and must have been gratified to discover so much in the way of the decorative arts that could not be found in Albany. He bought silver, hardware, glassware, fabrics, wallpapers, and carpets and shipped it all home. An "Invoice of Sundries Sent to America" itemizes Schuyler's purchases of flocked wallpaper in green, blue, yellow, and crimson along with borders and a "neat Mache Ceiling to plan for room 26 ft by 20"purchased from William Squire. A scenic wallpaper described as the "Ruins of Rome" was reserved for the hall. Although the original wallpapers did not survive into the 20th century, this original documentation provides the information needed to reproduce the wallpapers installed in the house today. Work is currently in progress at Schuyler Mansion to restore it to its condition in the 1790s.

OPPOSITE *Of all the bedchambers, the southeast Master Chamber, used by Philip and Catherine Schuyler, is clearly the most elaborate and includes paneled walls and a decorative cornice. A green flocked paper, painted green walls, and a Brussels carpeting have been installed to reflect the 1790s period of the Schuyler residency. The mahogany chest-on-chest in the corner was probably made in New England c. 1770-1780. The circa 1795-1800 transitional Chippendale-Hepplewhite chairs descended in the Schuyler family.*

Serving as a guest chamber as well as the bedroom of the Schuylers, this room housed defeated British General John "Gentleman Johnny" Burgoyne following the Battle of Saratoga. Schuyler offered his home to Burgoyne after no suitable place could be found for the General to have the "time and solitude" that he requested in order to write to the British government. According to Baroness Riedsel, who along with her husband accompanied Burgoyne, when the British General thanked Schuyler, Schuyler responded "That is the fate of war—let us say no more about it." During the ten days he stayed at the mansion, Burgoyne occupied himself with an account of the battle and other correspondence, probably remaining in this chamber to write. Along with him was his staff and "personal suite," some of whom likely stayed in this same room. As a token of his appreciation for the hospitality presented to him, he presented his rhinestone shoe buckles as a gift to Schuyler's daughter. They are on exhibit in the site's Visitor Center.

OPPOSITE BOTTOM *An excellent example of trapunto quiltwork with a central pineapple motif and scroll borders covers the corner bed. Writings by Schuyler refer to his daughter staying in this northeast bed chamber across the hall from his own room.*

RIGHT *With just four bedrooms on the second floor, a large family, and numerous and frequent guests, doubling up of beds within each room would be common. Furnished for visiting grandsons, complete with a young man's clothing laid out on the bed, this room includes a field bed, (far end) which first came into popularity in America about 1780, although the style appeared in design books as early as 1762. The name comes either from a resemblance to the silhouette of an army officer's tent or from the ease of disassembling the frame, which made the bed easy to use in military situations. According to Sheraton, these beds were suitable for either servants or children.*

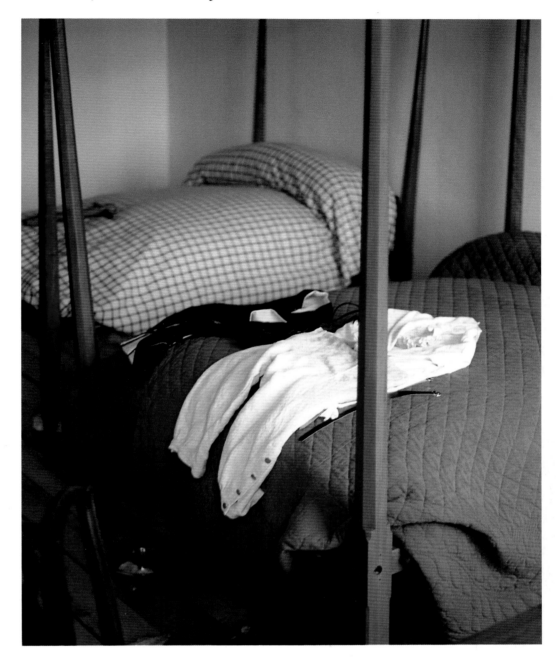

Philip and Catherine Schuyler lived at Schuyler Mansion with their eight children. Their visitor's book, had there been one, would have made interesting reading and included the names of George Washington, Benjamin Franklin, Benedict Arnold and many others. In 1777 following the defeat of the British under General John Burgoyne at the Battle of Saratoga, Burgoyne stayed as a prisoner and guest at Schuyler Mansion for ten days while the American troops guarding him camped on the property. In1780, Schuyler's daughter, Elizabeth, married Alexander Hamilton in the southeast parlor.

Catherine Van Rensselaer died in1803 and Philip Schuyler died a year later. Upon his death, and in accordance with his will, the land around Schuyler Mansion was divided into lots, giving birth to the densely packed urban streetscape that surrounds the house today. Schuyler Mansion was used as a private residence for years and then, from 1886 until 1914, as the St. Frances de Sales Orphan Asylum. Legislation was passed to provide funds for New York State to acquire and preserve the house, and following three years of restoration, Schuyler Mansion opened to the public as a historic house museum on October 17, 1917.

The Luykas Van Alen house consists of a two-room 1737 section with a window and front door opening into each room. Shortly thereafter another room and hall with exterior doors at either end were added to the north end of the house, accommodating an expanding family and slaves. The gable walls extended above the roofline to form a parapet, a Dutch building feature designed to make the roof more weathertight.

Luykas Van Alen House

In the colonial period, most of the land along the Hudson River was held in land speculators' patents or as manorial land grants whose owners tried to derive their income from farm and mill rentals. However, the more enterprising farmers, millers, and traders sought what freehold land they could get so that their improvements could be passed on to their heirs and not revert to landlords. In what is now Columbia County, available freehold land at Kinderhook attracted many Dutch families, who established prosperous mills and farms along the fertile creek flats in the late 17th century. One of the most successful of these settlers was Lourens Van Alen, proprietor of 17,000 acres at Kinderhook. His son Luykas Van Alen built a handsome brick house on what was the most highly valued farm on the tax rolls of the Kinderhook region. It has survived, through various branches of the Van Alen family, little altered, to become a museum of the Columbia County Historical Society in 1963, and a National Historic Landmark in 1968.

The Luykas Van Alen House, built in 1737, is a rare example of a particular Dutch colonial house type, characterized by distinctive brick parapets at the gable ends. Only a few American houses of this type have survived, and most of them are near Albany. Its form is derived from the vernacular houses of the Netherlands, which trace their antecedents to the medieval period. This medieval building type illustrates the use of Netherlands prototypes by New York housewrights of Dutch descent who, by 1737, were already three to four generations removed from their Netherlands ancestry. They continued to build in the 17th-century manner for nearly a century after the British took over the administration of New Netherland in 1664.

Characteristic architectural features of the Van Alen house included a load-bearing wood framing system, enveloped by a thin veneer of brick, fastened back to the wood frame with wrought-iron wall anchors decorated on the exterior façade with various ornamental designs, including the date of the building. At the gable ends the walls

RIGHT The date of the house, 1737, can be seen written out on the end wall of the house in the wrought iron anchors.

ABOVE The Dutch open fireplace has no sides or jambs, unlike the conventional English fireplace. A large hoodlike chimney above captured the smoke but drew off so much air it increased cold drafts. While inefficient for winter heating, the draft helped cool the room in summer. The openness of a fire gives out a wide glow to a room enhancing its visual appeal, an attraction that helps explain its persistence among the Dutch long after the more efficient, smaller, English jambed fireplace was known to them.

RIGHT The Dutch fireplace consisted of a suspended mantel molding enclosing the bottom of the wide chimney. To ensure that smoke would find its way upward, and not into the room, the Dutch further suspended a cloth below head-height. The blue floral-and-vine pattern of this cloth copies early examples popular among the New World Dutch.

were carried above the roofline to form a straight parapet, with bricks angled into triangles that the Dutch called *vlechtegen* or braidwork. The steeply pitched roof and the parapet were built to make the roof more watertight and to give the house its architectural character.

Within, the house was detailed in the Dutch medieval tradition. The wooden frame posts were openly expressed and joined by braces, called *corbelen*, to large smooth-planed ceiling beams, the largest of which carried the weight of the chimney. The fireplaces were large and open, and unlike later English fireplaces, had no sides or jambs. The Dutch builders self-consciously held on to their traditional culture in this upriver region, including their ancient house forms, until the end of the last French and Indian War, in 1763, after which English fashions were widely adopted. At the Van Alen house fireplaces were rebuilt in the English manner by the time

RIGHT North room (addition). The rooms of Dutch houses, no matter how they were furnished and used, were built the same, with a Dutch fireplace, windows, and an exterior door. When this room was added to the house its use, judging by records of such additions in many other houses, was most likely as a summer kitchen and servants (and slaves) residence. The sparseness of furnishing today accurately reflects the dearth of objects listed in most early inventories.

BELOW Decorative columns of Dutch Delftware tiles mark the width of the Dutch fireplace. These examples depict children's games. Archaeological excavation has demonstrated that the Van Alens, like other Dutch families in the 18th century, more commonly used blue-and-white tiles of biblical events which reminded the Dutch of their faith and scriptural parallels to their own experiences. In the New World they thought of themselves, in the biblical sense, as a "remnant in the wilderness."

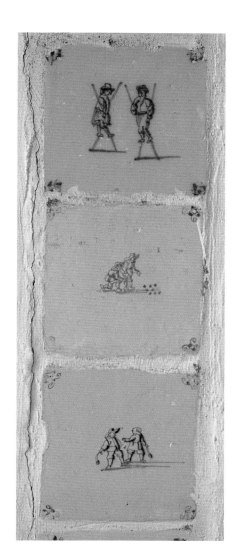

of the American Revolution and were restored to their original form only recently.

Other features of the house reflected traditional Dutch building practices. Large casement windows provided illumination for daytime work. "Dutch" doors acted like window shutters and regulated light and temperature, and the coming and going of children, visitors, and animals. The open garret above was used for storage, including seed grain for the next planting, for work space, and for overflow sleeping quarters. Cellar rooms held stored produce and another fireplace, perhaps for use by the servants.

As built in 1737, the house had two rooms, a kitchen and *groote kamer*, or great room, each with its own front door and fireplace. What distinguished the kitchen from the great room was the furnishings, not the architecture, for the rooms were nearly identical. Both contained beds (the Dutch lived on one floor) but the great room was reserved for special occasions, while the kitchen was used for everyday family life, cooking, and eating.

The Van Alens outgrew their house and built an addition, creating a hall and an extra room. The hall was a new idea to the Dutch in this region but proved useful. It allowed for greater separation of rooms, improved circulation and more comfort and privacy, and was characteristic of the English-style houses that would supersede the Dutch in the

upper Hudson River Valley. It was a common Dutch practice to add an additional room, almost always motivated by a desire for increased privacy and comfort. More rooms allowed for the separation of hot summer cooking and the activities of servants and slaves (the Van Alens had several) from the family rooms. More rooms might also create space for an expanding household, and allow a succeeding son and his family to share the house with his parents.

The Columbia County Historical Society's collection of period furnishings at the Van Alen House reflects Dutch domestic life in a rural community. Objects that relate to work, food preparation, child rearing, storage, and cloth production are part of the interpretation of this historic house museum. An 18th-century baby walker, a Dutch *kas* and *pottebank*, and a

OPPOSITE Two views in the south or great room. The groote kamer, *or great chamber, was reserved for special occasions, although the parents usually slept there. The finest textiles, paintings, furniture, and decorative earthenware were found in this room, as well as a* kas, *or cupboard, for the storage of valuables like silver and linens. One Dr. Alexander Hamilton in 1744 observed of the Dutch around Albany, "They affect pictures much, particularly scripture history, with which they adorn their rooms. They set out their cabinets and buffets much with china."*

BELOW RIGHT The Van Alen Farm, a restoration plan. Luykas Van Alen's house was the center of a large farm which derived its income primarily from the sale of field crops like wheat but which also produced food for the family and its servants, including slaves who primarily worked the farm. The house, then as now, faced the roadway and to the rear, around the barnyard, were located the common structures of Dutch farms. The largest structure was a Dutch barn in which cattle and horses found shelter and the year's grain crops were stored. One or more hay barracks, consisting of a conical roof raised and lowered on stout poles, sheltered hay for winter feed for the stock. A corn crib protected and dried corn cobs. A slant-roof shed was used as a workplace for various farm activities which might include weaving, carpentry, or blacksmithing as well as tool storage. Close to the house was the kitchen garden, the farm wife's personal domain for raising vegetables, medicinal herbs, and flowers. Close by were shelters for chickens, sheep, pigs, and bees. Beyond the fences, which kept stock within the barnyard and out of the gardens, were fields of grain, peas, and corn, and wood lots sufficient for winter heating and cooking fires.

Luykas Van Alen Farmstead

Hudson Valley Dutch loom are valuable examples of colonial Dutch furnishings.

Seven generations of the Van Alen family lived in the house into the 1930s. The house was donated to the Columbia County Historical Society in 1963, which undertook restoration work and the acquisition of furniture to allow for the interpretation of Dutch colonial farm life. The Society continues to maintain the building as a historic site open to the public in the summer months.

Lindenwald

Lindenwald is of interest as the one-time home of President Martin Van Buren, and as an illustration of the changes in architectural taste and fashion that take place over the years.

In 1786, General Peter Van Ness, a veteran of the French and Indian Wars and the American Revolution, purchased a parcel of land near Kinderhook and for a time lived in the stone house that stood there. This house he later replaced with the present one, a brick, center-hall Georgian, five bays wide. It was a simple house and a little old-fashioned at the time it was built. When it was put up for sale in 1839, the newspapers described it as "a plain, substantial, commodious house, built in the year 1797, of the best materials, and with more regard to comfort than show." William Van Ness inherited the house in 1804. He practiced law and, like his father, became a judge. He was Aaron Burr's second in Burr's notorious duel with Alexander Hamilton. It was from Van Ness that Martin Van Buren received his early legal education. In 1824, Van Ness lost the house to creditors, and in 1839 Van Buren bought it along with 137 acres.

Van Buren bought it intending to retire to Kinderhook one day. He was born there in 1782, the son of a tavern owner. He apprenticed to Francis Sylvester at fourteen and was admitted to the bar at age twenty-one. He rose rapidly through the ranks of local, state and national politics, served as United States Senator, Governor of New York, and Secretary of State. He was Vice-President under his mentor, Andrew Jackson, and was elected President in 1837. Van Buren's term began just as the nation suffered a severe economic downturn. In 1840, he lost his bid for reelection to William Henry Harrison, and in 1844 lost the Democratic Party's nomination to James Polk. He returned to Kinderhook and in 1848 he ran for President on the Free Soil ticket, after which he retired from active politics, although he remained an influential advisor.

Lindenwald was acquired by the National Park Service in 1974 to commemorate the life and work of Martin Van Buren, the nation's eighth president. The house has been restored to its mid-19th-century appearance, and work has begun on the restoration and protection of the cultural landscape. In Van Buren's time, there was a romantic formal area in front of the house, consisting of a black locust allée, symmetrical gatehouses, a rustic lawn, and a promenade. (The photograph at left shows the front lawn as seen from the Upjohn porch).

ABOVE From his library desk Van Buren managed his farm and conducted an extensive correspondence with friends and important political leaders. In his initial years at Lindenwald Van Buren was quite active in national politics both in pursuit of political office and as an advisor. The decorative effects in this room reflect the mid-century Upjohn aesthetic.

RIGHT A bust of Van Buren by Hiram Powers, said to be the best likeness of Van Buren in any medium.

Van Buren thought of his property as a gentleman's farm where he could pursue his interest in horticulture. He changed the name from Kleinrood to Lindenwald and began to make improvements to what had become, since Van Ness's tenure, a run-down estate. While still in Washington, he arranged for the construction of stables, a hothouse, fishponds, and an extensive orchard.

In 1849 Smith Van Buren came to live with his father at Lindenwald and received his father's permission to make extensive changes to accommodate his family. Van Buren wrote, "Smith made it an indispensable condition that he should be permitted to add sufficient to my House to make as many rooms as he may want without entering upon what I now have. I at first rejected this as impracticable without detriment to the appearance of the old House. But he & his wife have been to New York to consult with the great architectural oracle…" The oracle was Richard Upjohn, and it was he who designed the transformation of Lindenwald from a simple Georgian house into an Italianate villa.

Richard Upjohn was born in Shaftesbury, England, in 1802, the son of a surveyor. As a boy, he was apprenticed to a cabinetmaker and later set up shop for himself. He married and had a son, fell into debt, and in 1829 sailed with his family to America. He made his way to New Bedford where he worked as a draftsman and soon began to style himself as an architect. By 1834 he was living in Boston, working for Alexander Parris and taking commissions on the side. It was a stroke of good luck for Upjohn that a client, Dr. Jonathon Wainwright, was called to New York to become the rector at Trinity Church. At Dr. Wainwright's suggestion, Trinity engaged Upjohn to prepare designs for major structural repairs, and when it was determined that these would be insufficient, to prepare designs for a new church building. It was this commission, begun in 1839 and completed in 1846, which led to Upjohn's fame and fortune and paved the way for a penniless cabinetmaker to become the nation's leading ecclesiastical architect and the founding president of the American Institute of Architects.

In 1849, three years after his triumph at Trinity Church, Upjohn was working on the proposed alterations to Lindenwald. His designs were completed in 1850 and, by the end of 1851, the transformation was complete. The Van Burens must have been pleased. Smith Van Buren was a founding member of St. Paul's Episcopal Church in Kinderhook, and in 1851, Upjohn was commissioned to design a new church for the congregation.

Van Buren died in 1862, by which time Smith Van Buren had lost interest in Lindenwald. Ownership fell to his brother John, who sold it in 1864. Since then, the house changed owners many times, and was used variously as a residence, nursing home, tea house, and antiques shop.

Architectural fashion changed too. At the end of the 19th century, the Victorian styles fell out of favor and gave way to a renewed interest in neoclassical architecture, in particular early American architecture. Upjohn's biographer, his great-grandson Everard Upjohn, wrote of Lindenwald in 1939, "The change in character of a good colonial house cannot but be deplored by any lover of the older forms of American architecture." Another writer in 1942 described Upjohn's alterations as the "regret-

ABOVE *Lindenwald's formal parlor saw visits from such political luminaries as Henry Clay and Thomas Hart Benton. To either side of the ogee arch are fellow Democrats Thomas Jefferson and Andrew Jackson. Over the mantel is "the Red Fox of Kinderhook" himself, Martin Van Buren.*

LEFT *Behind the mansion stretched a large working farm. There Van Buren experimented with progressive agricultural methods and supervised farm workers, growing much of the produce to support the large household and sending a considerable amount to market. The Van Buren farm is now protected land that has been leased to an organic farmer in order to preserve its historic appearance.*

table" changes made to "an admirable piece of late Georgian architecture." In the 1950s one of the owners went so far as to add a neo-classical portico, inspired by George Washington's Mount Vernon, in an attempt to mask Lindenwald's Italianate appearance. In our own less orderly time, we have a greater appreciation of mid-19th-century architecture and enjoy its charm and eccentricities, and on occasion, its beauty.

RIGHT *In his sunny bedchamber in the southeast corner of Lindenwald, Martin Van Buren spent the last few days of his life, lapsing in and out of consciousness to inquire about the course of the Civil War. He died on July 24, 1862, not knowing if the nation to which he had dedicated his life would survive.*

BELOW *The chamber pictured below was used by Martin Van Buren's son Abraham and his wife, Angelica Singleton. The original of the portrait of Angelica is in the Red Room of the White House. Because Van Buren was a widower in the presidency, Angelica, a South Carolina belle and a cousin of Dolly Madison, served as his hostess.*

Van Buren himself observed the changes of fashion with detached amusement. He wrote, "Old Mr. Van Ness built as fine a home here as any reasonable man could…and its taste of what was then deemed the best. William P. came and disfigured every thing his father had done. I succeed him, and pulled down without a single exception any erection he had made & with evident advantage. Now comes Smith & pulls down many things I had put up and made the alterations without stint. The four operations will cost nearer fifty than forty thousand dollars for the buildings alone. What nonsense."

One more round of alterations occurred when, in 1974, the National Park Service bought Lindenwald and 22 acres to create the Martin Van Buren National Historic Site. Additions made since 1862 were removed and the house and grounds restored to the period when Martin Van Buren lived there.

Martin Van Buren National Historic Site, a unit of the National Park Service, is located on Route 9H, just south of the village of Kinderhook, New York. Its agricultural setting remains very much the same as it was during President Van Buren's ownership due to cooperative conservation efforts by private individuals and organizations and the foresight of Town, County, State and National Park Service land managers. The National Park Service is currently in the process of restoring the cultural landscape of the farm in accordance with an extensive *Cultural Landscape Report* and *Cultural Landscape Treatment Plan*.

There has been a Bronck home at the base of the Kalkberg not far from the western shore of the Hudson River close by Coxsachie Creek for nearly 340 years. The Bronck dwellings are situated on the crest of a plain which gently slopes away from the houses to the north and east. The older of the two, now joined, dwellings is the simple one-room rubble stone structure built by Pieter Bronck in 1663, believed to be the oldest surviving dwelling in the Hudson Valley. The large three-story brick veneer Dutch dwelling built by Pieter's grandson Leendert in 1738 is elegant by comparison and evidence of the family's increasing prominence and prosperity. The house is at the center of a cluster of barns including a New World Dutch barn and an extremely rare thirteen-sided barn (see photograph page 41).

Bronck Museum

Pieter Bronck was born in the province of Smoland, Sweden, around 1616, and was very likely a relation of Jonas Bronck, the Swede who came, via the Netherlands, to New Amsterdam and gave his name to the area where he settled, the Bronx. Pieter Bronck, like Jonas Bronck, was a sailor and was one of three men who assisted in 1643 with the evaluation of Jonas Bronck's estate. Several months later, back in the Netherlands, he married a Dutch woman named Hillitje Jans and by 1649 they were living together at Beverwyck, later known as Albany.

Pieter Bronck became a brewer in Albany, and received permission in 1651 to operate a tavern there. In 1661, three years before the English assumed control of New Netherland, he mortgaged his property and bought a tract of land from the Catskill Indians. The parchment deed transferring title was signed at Fort Orange on January 13, 1662. Bronck, short of cash at the time, agreed to pay 150 guilders in beaver skins, "one half when he shall come to live there, and the other half on the first day of May A.D 1663." The site was known as Koxhackhung, near the present-day village of Coxsackie, in what was then the wilderness south of Albany. In May of 1662, Bronck and his wife moved there and began the hard work of clearing the land, and on August 5, 1662, Bronck sold his houses, brewery, mill, and stables in Albany and paid off his mortgage the same day.

Bronck began the construction of his house in 1663. Built in the vernacular style common to the Netherlands, Germany, Scandinavia, and northern France, it was a simple twenty-foot square, single room structure, with a cellar and a garret. A wood frame of beams and rafters to support a steeply pitched roof topped the rubble stone

The massive original 17th-century hand hewn pine beams and sixteen-inch-wide floor planks held in place with huge hand-wrought nails remain in place and still define the interior of the 1663 dwelling of Pieter Bronck. In this single room, once heated and dimly lit by a primitive jambless fireplace, Pieter and his family carried on their everyday life. Food preparation and consumption, sleeping, and all farm, personal and family functions were carried on in this small space.

As the decades rolled into centuries changes in wealth, lifestyle, technology, and the addition of more living space made new demands on old spaces. The original jambless fireplace was replaced in the late 18th century with a more heat efficient and fashionable English-style jambed fireplace. The number and type of furnishings changed as well. In the 17th century the few furnishings were likely to have been crude and homemade. By the early 18th century, well-made storage pieces like the large Dutch kas, or cupboard, began to appear. A kas was often a part of a woman's dowry and a major addition to the furnishings of any reasonably prosperous Dutch home. Luxury items including portraits and religious art were possessed by a few rural families. Upriver Dutch families that were conservative and pious considered paintings with religious content to be

especially suitable for display in their homes. Artists working in the area around Albany in the early 18th century produced a group of religious paintings now referred to as scripture paintings. Each painting depicted a biblical parable. Often the artist would simply copy illustrations directly from Dutch Bibles. The scripture painting which hangs over the fireplace here was done by an unknown artist sometime around 1740 and depicts the Transfiguration of Christ.

walls. The original wooden "bones" of Pieter Bronck's house remain in place today. The massive, hand-hewn cellar beams still support wide floor boards, secured with 17th-century nails, and a floor hatch to the cellar still opens on the original 17th-century hinges. The dimensions of the first floor beams indicate that a huge fireplace once occupied most of the western wall. It is said that Pieter Bronck's house, which has stood for nearly 340 years, is the oldest surviving Dutch house in the Hudson River Valley.

Bronck died in 1669. The entry in the deacon's account book of the Albany Dutch Church reads, "2 skipples of wheat from the widow of Pieter Bronck for the pall." He left the house and farm to his widow and their son, Jan Bronck, who in turn left it to his son, Leendert Bronck. While his father was still alive, Leendert must have felt the need to have a house of his own and arranged to have a sizable new dwelling built, ten feet to the north of the old stone house.

The second house, which was known in the Bronck family as "the New House," is more elegant than the primitive house of 1663. It bears the date "Ano 1738" and is thus roughly contemporary with the Van Alen house in Kinderhook with which it shares many of the characteristics of the classic Hudson Valley Dutch style. The house's rosy brick walls are laid up in English bond, with a parapet at each gable end. A sturdy post-and-beam frame, supporting the weight of the floors and roof, wraps around the center chimney. Both the first and second floor are divided into two spacious rooms, while the third floor garret is one large open space. The house is brightly lit and well ventilated by ten casement windows, and on the main floor, the rooms each have their own entrance through divided "Dutch" doors. When completed, this house was connected to the old stone house by means of an enclosed passageway known as the "hyphen hallway."

The two joined dwellings became the hub of Leendert Bronck's thriving farm. Commercial success, political position, and strategic marriages, including Leendert's own with Anna De Wandelaer, secured for the Bronck family a prominent position in the social life of the upper Hudson Valley. Leendert's son, Jan L. Bronck, and his son Leonard, were men of consequence in their community. During the upheaval of the

The hallways of the Bronck houses were constructed as connectors joining the older dwellings to subsequent additions. The top view is the interior of the Hyphen Hallway constructed in the first half of the 18th century to connect the 1663 and 1738 dwellings. In this space the north stone wall of the 1663 dwelling faces the white painted brick south wall of the 1738 dwelling. The hyphen hall was a much traveled space at the nexus of the household, providing access from either the front or the back of the house to the interior of both dwellings. This space contains four early molded panel Dutch doors. All have massive pinned frames and 18th-century hinges.

The rear hallway is located in the west wing, a stone addition built behind the first dwelling. The doorway at the back of the hall passes through the original rear wall of the 1663 dwelling and provides the only access to the early house from the new west wing. The framing of this portion of the house is essentially the same as that of the earlier structure although somewhat less massive. The exposed pine beams retain traces of early blue-green paint. The exterior Dutch doors at each end of this hall are sheathed with diagonal beaded boards and have original hardware. The stairway gives access to the second floor storage area of the west wing, and a doorway in the paneled wall below the stairs provides the interior entrance to the large cellar under the west wing. During the 17th and early 18th centuries nearly two thirds of the interior volume of the Bronck dwellings was given over to the storage of farm produce and the family food supply. To facilitate the movement of cumbersome and heavy items into the storage areas above and below the first floor living space, entrances to storage areas were located together and adjacent to exterior doorways.

Furnishings in the rear hallway are late 18th and early 19th century. Some are Bronck family pieces, including the handsome Chippendale pie-crust tilt-top table. Others, like the English tall case clock brought to Catskill by David Stead in 1812, were owned by families from neighboring communities. By the early 19th century the rural homes of prosperous families like the Broncks were furnished with a mix of American furniture, some new, some old, some high style and some country. As their wealth increased, and imported furniture became more available, these families desired and soon acquired the occasional piece of imported furniture to add luster to their rooms and impress the neighbors.

American Revolution they associated themselves with the American cause and in 1775 were signatories of the Coxsackie Declaration that supported the Continental Congress. Both were local judges, and Leonard served five years in the New York State Assembly, followed by eight in the New York State Senate.

When Jan L. Bronck died in 1794, Leonard Bronck became the fifth generation to own the farm at Coxsackie, where he lived with his own large family, his stepmother and several slaves. Like his forebears, he prospered, and in 1800 the farm was listed as the most valuable property on the county tax rolls. Leonard continued with improvements to the houses and the surrounding farm that had been started during his father's later years. He built a large new "Dutch" barn and a kitchen dependency and in the house removed the old fireplaces and installed handsome Georgian paneling.

By the dawn of the 19th century the Bronck family was very prosperous, well educated, and increasingly sophisticated. The dining-room occupies the majority of the space in the west wing. The furniture in this room belonged to the family. Much of the surviving Bronck furniture is fine quality solid mahogany and of American manufacture, in styles from Sheraton through Empire to late Victorian. The dining room furniture is primarily Sheraton in style. The Bronck dining table is a ten-foot-long expanse of burnished mahogany. The fall front bookcase desk is one of three surviving Bronck desks. Family china, silver, and glass fill cupboards throughout the room. The rare reticulated Staffordshire fruit basket, with matching tray on the third shelf of the bookcase desk, and the impressive Sèvres compote at the center of the dining table are both family pieces. Visible through the hall doorway is a portrait of Leonard Bronck, Jr., 1797-1872, son of Judge Bronck and the sixth generation Bronck owner.

He replaced the old Dutch casements with double-hung sashes, and repainted the old red and gray-blue walls with fashionable soft yellows and greens in order to make a congenial backdrop for his handsome new Federal furniture. With his substantial wealth Leonard Bronck might have built an entirely new house, but chose instead to gently "modernize" the old ones, an indication of the power of the traditions that bound him to the place his family had called home for the previous 160 years. In the dwellings of his forefathers Leonard raised a family, lived a long, productive life, and at its conclusion in 1828, left his property to his son.

The Bronck family owned the farm for three more generations. Their farming income allowed for a comfortable and privileged way of life. Sons attended college and daughters finishing school. The Broncks traveled abroad and enjoyed much of the best of American life during the late 19th and early 20th centuries. In 1939, after eight generations and 276 years of unbroken family ownership, Pieter's descendant, Leonard Bronck Lampman, a life-long bachelor, gave the house and barns to the Greene County Historical Society. The property is now a National Historic Landmark and operated as a historic house museum by the Greene County Historical Society.

OPPOSITE *Interior of the house built in 1738 by Leendert Bronck. The heavy post-and-beam construction, and scrubbed wide-plank flooring confirm the age of this dwelling. Everywhere in the Bronck houses layers of time are heaped one upon another. The corner space now occupied by a tall case clock was the original location of a Dutch box bed. This now elegantly furnished room was simultaneously kitchen, bedroom, and farm office in the 18th century. The furnishings in this room are family pieces spanning the entire 19th century. Some of the room's more notable furnishings are the earlier pieces. The tall case made in England by Cauldwell and Worley was purchased by the family in 1802. Immediately adjacent to the clock is the Ezra Ames portrait of the most prominent of the Bronck men and the fifth generation owner Judge Leonard Bronck, 1751-1828. Hanging over the family's Gilbert piano organ is one of a matching pair of imposing convex mirrors dating to the first quarter of the 19th century. The reflected image of the room's east wall including the Dutch door and the Ammi Phillips' portrait of Elsie Salisbury is caught in the mirror.*

RIGHT *By the beginning of the 19th century Judge Leonard Bronck had begun to "modernize" this portion of the dwelling, changing window position and sash, and replacing the original jambless fireplace with a conventional jambed fireplace and Federal mantel. The 18th-century cast-iron fireback bearing the coat of arms of Great Britain survived the alterations and remains in place.*

Olana

Frederic Edwin Church was born in Hartford, Connecticut in 1826, the son of a well-to-do insurance agent who encouraged him in his pursuit of an artistic career. From 1844 to 1846 he studied with Thomas Cole, the founder of the Hudson River School of painting, and in 1847 opened his own studio in New York and began to paint the great landscapes that made his reputation. He traveled in search of ever more exotic scenery and held public shows of his luminous views of the wonders of North and South America, such as "Niagara" in 1857, and "Heart of the Andes" in 1859. It was at this last exhibition that he met Isabel Mortimer Carnes, whom he married in 1860. They were an extremely attractive, charismatic couple and Church was at the height of his fame. It is said that when they arrived at the opera, the audience would break into applause.

To escape from the acclaim, and to paint and raise a family, Church bought a farm with spectacular views of the Hudson River, views he had painted during his days with Thomas Cole, whose studio was directly across the Hudson River in Catskill. Church hired Richard Morris Hunt, the architect of the Tenth Street Studio building where Church painted in New York, and commissioned him to design a small house, later called "Cosy Cottage." Church then turned his attention to the cultivation of his farm. He kept the original owner on as manager and built new farm buildings, ten in all by 1867. As one might expect, the great landscape painter developed an interest in landscape design and began to plant trees, composing the views and vistas from his cottage much as he did on canvas.

Church's farm included everything but the hilltop on which he hoped to build. He was able to buy it in 1867, at a premium, and asked Hunt to prepare plans for a new house. Church must have formed by then many of his ideas about the design, for Hunt's elevations indicated polychromatic, patterned brick work and many other elements used later in the final design. But the scheme was unconvincing, and Church put it aside, leaving on an extended trip that took him, his wife and their infant son to Europe and the Middle East. In London, Church met many of the artists and architects of the Aesthetic Movement, perhaps including Frederic Leighton, the artist whose Holland Park house, with its picture galleries and exotic, polychromatic decoration bears a strong resemblance to the spirit of Olana. Church and his family

ABOVE *Aerial view of the main house at Olana with the Hudson River and Catskill Mountains to the west. This is almost the same view as depicted in Church's painting below.*

BELOW *Frederic Church, "Catskill Mountains from the Home of the Artist," 1871.*

RIGHT *The northwest corner of the studio depicting Church's easel and paint stand, the wooden window screen pierced with a Middle Eastern design, "Ira Mountain, VT" painted by Church in 1850, the carved teakwood mantel from the workshop of Lockwood de Forest, and a variety of Middle Eastern textiles.*

The focus of the sitting room is Church's "El Khasné Petra," and the colors of the painting are reflected in the fireplace surround and Arabic calligraphy in the wall stencils. In the corner are Church's sketches for two of his most famous works, "Niagara Falls" and "Twilight in the Wilderness," and a portrait of his wife Isabel.

traveled to the Middle East where they stayed for six months. From his exposure there to Islamic architecture Church finally sensed the form for Olana.

On his return, Church replaced Hunt with the architect Calvert Vaux. Church wanted to be his own designer, something the imperious Hunt would never tolerate. The referral may have come from Church's pupil, Jervis McEntee, who was Vaux's brother-in-law. Vaux came to America from England in 1850 to be the architectural assistant to Andrew Jackson Downing, and when Downing died in 1852, set up his own architectural practice. By 1870, Vaux was a seasoned designer of picturesque villas, and more to the point, was more patient and flexible than Hunt. After all, he had worked successfully with the brilliant but difficult Frederick Law Olmsted, collaborating on the designs for New York's Central Park and Brooklyn's Prospect Park.

Church was clearly the designer of Olana, but Vaux's role was important. His initial design, done in May of 1870, was far more successful than Hunt's scheme. Vaux was a better designer of the type of house Church intended to build, and Hunt's great success would come later, with the palatial houses he built in the 1880s and 1890s for the Vanderbilts on Fifth Avenue and at Newport. Church used Vaux's elevations and massing, but moved the towers around, and inspired by his numerous books on

ABOVE *The east end of the Court Hall showing glimpses into the dining room, vestibule, and East parlor.*

architecture, completely worked over the design and details of the patterned brick elevations.

The masons began building the thick walls in May of 1870, with Church in command, and by the summer of 1873 the family was living on the second floor, trying their best to stay out of the way of the carpenters working on the first. Church took charge of the decoration of the interiors, mixed paint colors and designed the stenciled ornament. He artfully placed the furniture, decorative objects, and paintings. By 1877, Church could fairly boast, "I designed the house myself. It is Persian in style adapted to the climate and requirements of modern life. The interior decorations and fittings are all in harmony with the external architecture." He called his house Olana, an English translation of a Greek word, *Olane.*

As time went on and tastes changed, Church's popularity declined and he was increasingly afflicted with arthritis. It is understandable that he turned more and more to the design of his house and grounds. Working in the tradition of English pictur-

48

esque landscape design and the American work of Vaux and Olmsted, he planted thousands of trees, creating a contrast between these and the broad pastoral vistas that they formed. Church laid out miles of roads and dredged a marsh to create a ten-acre lake. Understandably proud of his efforts, he wrote, "I can make more and better landscapes in this way than by tampering with canvas and paint in the studio."

However, he did not give up painting altogether, and enjoyed sketching his house and grounds. In 1888, he began construction of the studio wing, for which he prepared the architectural designs, and wrote, in April of 1891, "I inaugurated the New Studio—it is perfect. Filled with enthusiasm I attacked my first canvas and an Iceberg scene is the result, the best I think I have ever painted and the truest."

Isabel Church died in 1899, and Frederic Church a year later. Their heirs owned Olana until 1964 when they made plans to auction the property. Olana Preservation, Inc., formed by art historian David C. Huntington, purchased the 250-acre property in 1966 with the assistance of New York State. Soon afterward, New York State took title, opened the house and grounds to the public as the Olana State Historic Site, and saved for the future one of the nation's unique artistic treasures.

A view of the northwest corner of the Court Hall featuring a combination of Middle Eastern brass work, Aesthetic Movement furniture, oriental ceramics and Middle Eastern textiles.

Clermont

LEFT AND ABOVE: The west façade of Clermont: The front entry to Clermont faces the Hudson River. The original Georgian home was enlarged several times during the 19th century. The steep-pitched slate Chateauesque roof was added in 1874.

Robert Livingston was born in Scotland in 1654 but moved to the Netherlands as a boy. His father, the Rev. John Livingston, a Presbyterian minister and a man of strong convictions, was exiled there for refusing to pledge his allegiance to Charles II and the Anglican Bishops and died there in 1672. The following year Robert Livingston sailed to the New World and made his way to Albany, at the time a small fur-trading town dominated by the Van Rensselaer and Schuyler families. Livingston was charming, ambitious, and fluent in Dutch, and became in a year's time secretary of the town of Albany, secretary to the Board of Indian Commissioners, and secretary to Nicholas Van Rensselaer, Director of Rensselaerswyck, the vast patroonship that encompassed the present-day counties of Albany and Rensselaer.

In 1678, Van Rensselaer died. Eight months later, Livingston married his widow, Alida Schuyler Van Rensselaer, and took his place among Albany's insular Dutch establishment. Livingston and his wife made a claim upon Van Rensselaer's estate and the patroonship and used this claim as leverage to secure a royal patent for 160,000 acres in what is now Columbia County. In this way Robert Livingston became First Lord of Livingston Manor and the founder of a great American family, one that would dominate the social, political, and economic life of the upper Hudson River Valley for years to come. When he died in 1728, he left Livingston Manor to his son

Philip. He also set aside 13,000 acres, called the Lower Manor, for his third son, Robert, who built a house there in the 1750s in the newly fashionable Georgian style, comparable in many ways to Schuyler Mansion and Philipse Manor Hall. It became known as Claremont, and later, after the outbreak of war with England, Clermont.

In 1742 the rising star of the Livingstons of the Lower Manor began to rise faster when the First Lord's grandson, Judge Robert R. Livingston, married Margaret Beekman, daughter and only heir of Colonel Henry Beekman of Rhinebeck. Margaret Beekman brought to the marriage important social connections and a dowry of 240,000 acres in Dutchess County. Their ten children built many of the great houses that line the Hudson River below Clermont, including Montgomery Place, Edgewater, and Staatsburgh, and their eldest son, Robert R. Livingston, Jr., the heir to Clermont, became the most prominent Livingston of all.

The Livingstons supported the patriotic side during the American Revolution and found themselves uncomfortably situated between General Burgoyne's forces at Fort Ticonderoga and British-occupied Manhattan. In 1777 British troops under the command of General John Vaughan sailed up the Hudson and burned the city of Kingston, the same time that Burgoyne surrendered to the American forces at the Battle of Saratoga. Vaughan retreated to New York, but before he did, he made one last stop at Clermont and torched it. The widowed Margaret Beekman Livingston

ABOVE The dining room: Clermont's interior house furnishings were acquired by the Livingston family between 1730 and 1930. Thomas Sully's 1819 portrait of Andrew Jackson, a political ally of the Livingston family, occupies a place of honor in this room. Chancellor Livingston's Darte-Freres porcelain service is seen on the dining room table.

TOP RIGHT The drawing room [west view]: Guests at Clermont were formally received in this room, which is furnished with 18th- and 19th-century antiques. The balloon mantel clock, acquired by Chancellor Livingston while he was serving as American Minister to France, is based on a Houdon model for a commemorative statue depicting the flight of Charles and Robert in 1783.

RIGHT The drawing room [northeast view]: The square piano in this undated view was purchased by Edward P. Livingston circa 1810 from Broadwood and Sons of London.

rebuilt with the help of her slaves and her tenants, who were exempted from military service for this purpose by Governor George Clinton. By 1782 work was far enough along to allow her to entertain George and Martha Washington. She wrote her son Robert that the Washingtons had admired Clermont, but added, "I am obliged to leave my finishing the house for want of seasoned plank & an hand rail to finish my Stairs."

Robert R. Livingston, Jr., was born in New York in 1746. He was educated at King's College (Columbia University), studied law in the office of his cousin, William Livingston, and following admission to the New York bar formed a partnership with John Jay. Livingston was elected to the Second Continental Congress, helped draft the Declaration of Independence, and was appointed first Chancellor of New York State. In that capacity he administered the first oath of office to George Washington, but when Washington coolly rejected Livingston's application for high office, he broke with the

ABOVE *The library, located in the south wing of the mansion, was created by the architect Michael O'Connor during an 1893 remodeling of the house. Bookcases house a part of Chancellor Livingston's important private library. Alice Delafield Clarkson Livingston furnished the room with objects acquired in Italy during her family's residence in Florence in the 1920s.*

RIGHT *The library circa 1911. The room was originally dominated by John Henry Livingston's billiards table. After he married Alice Clarkson in 1906 the billiards table was removed and the room served as the family's living room.*

Federalist Party, allied himself with Thomas Jefferson and James Madison, and helped to found the new Jeffersonian Republican Party. In 1801 Jefferson sent him to Paris as Minister to France, where he aided Jefferson in negotiating the Louisiana Purchase.

Livingston was interested in the arts and the sciences. In New York, he and his brother Edward founded the American Academy of the Fine Arts, and in Paris, he became acquainted with Robert Fulton, a Pennsylvania-born painter and inventor. Their partnership resulted in America's first practical steamboat, which made its maiden voyage from New York City to Albany in 1807. Registered as North River, it was better known as the Clermont. In 1792, he began construction of a new house, just south of his mother's, known as New Clermont. The house was designed in the form of the letter H, with four one-story wings attached to the central block, and a greenhouse running the entire length of the south façade that was used as a banquet room on special occasions. It is possible that Livingston designed this house himself, referring to the books in his extensive library.

Chancellor Livingston died in 1813 and left New Clermont to his daughter Margaret Maria, and Old Clermont to his daughter Elizabeth. In 1814 Elizabeth and her husband, Edward Livingston, added a wing to the north side of Old Clermont, and, in 1831, a matching wing to the south. In 1874, their grandson, John Henry Livingston, added the steeply-pitched slate roof that gives the house its mid-19th century character.

In 1906 John Henry Livingston married Alice Delafield Clarkson, his third wife, and like him a descendant of Chancellor Livingston. They bought New Clermont from their cousins and reunited the original estate, but in 1909 it was engulfed in a fire, possibly caused by embers from a passing steam train. In the 1920s they decorated the interior of Old Clermont in the Colonial Revival style, in the spirit of Chancellor Livingston's era, and furnished it with a superb collection of portraits by Gilbert Stuart, Rembrandt Peale, and others. John Henry Livingston died in 1927, and, during the 1930s, Alice Livingston completed the formal gardens she had designed to the north and south of the house: the Cutting Garden, the Wilderness Garden, the Walled Garden, and the South Spring Garden. She incorporated the ruins of New Clermont into the landscape, and planted a lilac walk to connect them to the main house.

In 1962 at the age of ninety, Alice Livingston transferred ownership of the historic house, many of its furnishings, the carriage barn, and nearly 400 acres to the state of New York. Her daughter, Honoria Livingston McVitty, the last member of her family to live at Clermont, left additional acreage and family possessions. Clermont is preserved today much as it looked in the late 1920s and represents the long history of stewardship of seven generations of the Livingston family.

ABOVE AND LEFT *Spring views of the cutting garden and mansion environs: Mrs. John Henry Livingston created four formal gardens in the vicinity of the mansion between 1908 and 1935.*

Blithewood

Blithewood, which now occupies part of the campus of Bard College, was once part of a tract of land belonging to Pieter Schuyler of Albany, whose title to the property was confirmed by a patent granted in 1688. The upper portion of this land, in the vicinity of Red Hook, became first the property of Henry Beekman of Rhinebeck, and later of his daughter, Margaret, the wife of Robert R. Livingston of Clermont. In 1789 the Livingstons' daughter Alida married General John Armstrong, who once declared he was too proud to marry a woman with a fortune but too poor to marry a woman without one. Armstrong's poverty overcame his pride, and he extracted from the Livingstons a dowry that included 20,000 acres of the Schuyler Patent. The Armstrongs built a house just south of Tivoli, called The Meadows; a second, on the site of Blithewood, called Mill Hill; and a third, known today as Rokeby, where they finally settled.

John Cox Stevens bought Mill Hill in 1810. His family lived near the Livingstons in New York, and his father, Col. John Stevens, was Chancellor Robert Livingston's brother-in-law as well as his partner (and, later, competitor) in the development of steamboats. John Cox Stevens was the first commodore of the New York Yacht Club and a key member of the syndicate that built *America*, the yacht that in 1851 won the trophy that became the America's Cup. Stevens liked to design and build boats, and used the cove below his house as a boatyard. He also liked horse racing—he maintained a racing stable at Mill Hill—and was known for his extravagant wagers.

Robert Donaldson bought the estate in 1835 and renamed it Blithewood. He worked with his architect, Alexander J. Davis, to alter General Armstrong's old house and build numerous ornamental buildings around the grounds. Davis's 1836 design for a "rustic" gatehouse at Blithewood was illustrated in his book *Rural Residences*, whose publication Donaldson helped to finance. Davis designed a hexagonal gatehouse in 1841, a new wing for the main house in 1842, and a picture gallery in 1845. Over the years Davis designed a number of garden buildings, including an Egyptian revival toolhouse and a springhouse and bathhouse, a greenhouse, a rustic arbor, and numerous benches. Only the hexagonal gatehouse stands today.

Donaldson befriended Andrew Jackson Downing, the first American writer on landscape design. Donaldson was sophisticated and rich and a devotee of architectural and horticultural improvement, traits that were irresistible to Downing. He visited Donaldson at Blithewood, supplied him with plants from his greenhouses, and offered horticultural advice. Donaldson introduced Downing to Davis, who was persuaded to contribute sketches and designs to illustrate Downing's 1842 book, *Cottage Residences*, which Downing dedicated to Donaldson.

Donaldson was also friendly with Dr. David Hosack, a physician and a professor of botany at Columbia College. Donaldson was

PREVIOUS PAGES *The aerial view shows the garden façade, which was the view published in 1907. It shows the more formal traditional façade of the building rather than the side, which visitors saw first upon arriving from the formal entrance past a gatehouse to the porte-cochere. As a result of the house's orientation to the river, its residents saw the rolling hills as a background to the classical garden designed by Hoppin. A porch outside the living room led to a descending terrace from which one stepped down to the classical garden.* (INSET) *The garden as laid out by Mrs. Andrew C. Zabriskie, c. 1915.*

ABOVE LEFT *Entrance hall. The size of the hall is emphasized by the placement of the stair against the wall facing the garden.*

Woodwork is conceived in the classical idiom, with the fireplace richly embellished with relief ornament. The stair's wainscot is positioned high for the Colonial Revival style and the balusters on the stair resemble earlier work, but the white paint, which is original, makes the overall effect very up-to-date. The arched opening leads off the hall to the group of rooms that can be called parlors, which end in the large room the family called the living room. The gray color of the hall matches the color of the living room.

ABOVE *Living room. A grand room in revival style, inspired by Renaissance to Empire design. The doors flanking the fireplace lead to the porch with the river view and access to the classical garden.*

inspired by the English-style landscape that Hosack had created at the Hyde Park estate he bought in 1828 from Dr. Samuel Bard, his medical partner. In 1853, when Donaldson moved to Edgewater, Bard's grandson, John Bard, bought Blithewood. In 1860 Bard donated 18 acres of Blithewood and $60,000 for the construction of St. Stephen's College, a training school to prepare students to enter the General Theological Seminary of the Protestant Episcopal Church in New York. Over the years St. Stephen's became increasingly secular. It associated itself for a time with Columbia University, and in 1934 became Bard College.

Capt. Andrew Christian Zabriskie bought Blithewood in 1899. He was a descendant of Albrecht Zaborowsky, who had arrived in New Amsterdam via Prussia in 1662 and invested in large tracts of land in New Jersey that formed the foundation of his family's fortune. Captain Zabriskie attended West Point, was a National Guardsman, and organized the Blithewood Light Infantry, a group of local Red Hook men who

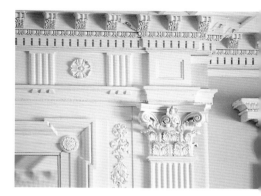

The blue parlor (left) and complementary pink parlor (opposite) were furnished in 18th-century revival designs, with occasional early pieces. The wall and fireplace decoration are in the 18th-century spirit, but in the style of about 1900, which is more elaborate than the earlier models. The Palladian windows are matching. In the pink parlor the bookcase is almost identical to the one that was originally in the room. In both rooms the furnishings capture the spirit of the original furnishings. The photographs above the bookcase, views of ancient monuments, are typical of those that gentlemen hung in their libraries at that time.

ABOVE The living room mantelpiece is enriched with a variety of classical revival moldings and fluted pilasters.

gathered to parade and practice military drills on the estate. He was an antiquarian, cattle breeder, and collector of political memorabilia, but his greatest passion was numismatics. From 1884 to 1905 he served as Vice President and then President of the American Numismatic and Archaeological Society; part of his coin collection is now in the Smithsonian Institution.

In 1901, Zabriskie engaged Francis L. V. Hoppin and his partner, Terrence A. Koen, to design a house and garden on the site of the existing house. Hoppin and Koen began their careers as rising stars in the architecture firm of McKim, Mead & White and went on to become architects of fashionable country houses, most notably Edith Wharton's Berkshire house, The Mount, which was built around the same time as Blithewood. Hoppin attended the Trinity Military Institute and had considered a military career before deciding to become an architect; it may have been their mutual interest in military affairs that made Hoppin and Captain Zabriskie sympatico. The Blithewood commission was a feather in Hoppin's cap as he was only thirty-three when Zabriskie called on him. The romantic age of architecture in the style of Downing and Davis was long gone, replaced by the "Gilded Age" and the revival of classical design that McKim, Mead & White, through their buildings, and Edith Wharton, through her writing, did so much to foster. Hoppin replaced Robert Donaldson's bracketed cottage with an impressive forty-two-room edifice, symmetrically massed and ornamented with an array of quoins, pilasters, pediments, urns, and venetian windows, all derived from English country houses of the 18th century.

Hoppin's siting of the house was peculiar. Instead of orienting the house to the west and the river view, as most architects did along the Hudson River, he turned it 90 degrees, presumably to maximize exposure to sunlight along the broad side of the

house. Perversely, however, he placed the entrance to the house on the south façade, leaving the principal rooms in shadow, looking out on the grounds to the north. Hoppin believed that "house and garden were properly part of a single design" and that a garden should be an "architectural garden." With these principles in mind, he designed a series of lawn terraces, on axis with the west façade of the house, that descend into an enclosed court decorated with statuary niches, parterres, and a fountain pool and terminate at a pergola and summerhouse overlooking the river and facing the mountains beyond.

Captain Zabriskie died in 1916, but his family enjoyed the use of Blithewood until 1951, when his son, Christian, donated the house and 825 acres to Bard College. Between 1986 and 1988 Bard renovated the house and adapted it for its current use as the home of The Jerome Levy Economics Institute of Bard College.

Montgomery Place

Janet Livingston was born on August 27, 1743, the oldest of ten children of Judge Robert R. Livingston and his wife Margaret Beekman. She grew up to be a sociable and intelligent young woman known for her strong opinions. Her family was prominent in society, business, and politics and her inheritance secure. Not surprisingly, she had many suitors, and in 1773 she married Captain Richard Montgomery, a dashing expatriate Anglo-Irishman.

After their marriage, the couple moved to a small house in Rhinebeck and began to build an estate on the nearby Hudson. But their happiness was short-lived, and Janet's life was changed forever by the events of 1775. The Revolutionary War began at Concord and Lexington in April and in June, Montgomery was appointed Brigadier General in the Continental Army. Shortly after, Janet's grandfather, Robert Livingston, died at Clermont, and in December her father died there also. Finally, on December 31, while leading the charge against Quebec, Richard Montgomery was shot and killed. At the age of thirty-two, Janet Montgomery was a widow and an heiress.

Sometime in the 1790s, Montgomery's nephew, William Jones, left Ireland to live with his aunt and became a kind of adopted son. He brought with him the Anglo-Irish love of country houses, and by 1799 Janet was writing, "Jones…is making my farm a paradice." In 1802, Janet Montgomery sold her Rhinebeck estate, Grasmere, to her sister Joanna. She wanted the money to build on the 242-acre farm she had bought near Red Hook. Janet wrote to her brother Robert, now minister to France, asking him for blueprints, telling him that "Jones has made me do this foolish thing, but he is so delighted it would be a pity to check him in the improving it."

Together they built a house, a rectangular box, six bays wide and four bays deep, built of fieldstone with a stucco coating and crowned by a classical balustrade. They called it Chateau de Montgomery. The only surviving image of it was sketched by the architect A. J. Davis in 1841. In many ways it resembled other houses built at the turn of the century such as Gracie Mansion, on the East River, built in 1799-1804, or Clermont as it looked in 1799. Janet and William landscaped the property, had a

ABOVE *Montgomery Place has a splendid setting overlooking the Hudson River and the Catskill Mountains in the distance.*

OPPOSITE *In the 1860s, A.J. Davis added a semicircular portico supported by elaborate composite columns. The design was inspired by the temple of Vesta in Tivoli, near Rome. Davis also designed the balustrade, urns, and the pots with their rams head detail. By the 1980s the house and particularly this porch had fallen into serious disrepair but was painstakingly restored by Historic Hudson Valley.*

Janet Montgomery's original dwelling was a plain federal style house of fieldstone covered with stucco, five bays on the east and six on the west. A.J. Davis transformed it into a Classical Revival masterpiece in two stages, first in the 1840s and the second in the 1860s. He added porches, wings, and classical detail, but did not alter the original core.

greenhouse constructed, and operated a nursery business, thereby competing with A.J. Downing's father's nursery in Newburgh. Janet Montgomery died in 1828, leaving most of her property, including the Chateau, to her brother Edward.

Edward Livingston was born in 1764, the youngest child of Judge Robert R. Livingston. He graduated from Princeton, and in 1788 married Mary McEvers. Like his brother Robert, he pursued a career in the law and politics, and in 1800, following Thomas Jefferson's election, was appointed District Attorney of New York. His troubles were just beginning. Shortly after his appointment, his wife died of scarlet fever, and in 1803 his clerk embezzled a large sum of money, for which Livingston became indebted.

In the wake of scandal, Edward left for New Orleans where, in 1805, he married nineteen-year-old Louise D'Avezac de Castera Moreau de Lassy, a fellow refugee in New Orleans. She was the daughter of a French planter and had escaped from the political turbulence in Haiti. Their daughter Coralie was born in 1806. Life must have been difficult for Edward and his young family, but Livingston persevered. He speculated in real estate and entered politics again, serving in the Louisiana State legislature and in 1822 the House of Representatives. He moved his wife and daughter to Washington, and about that time they began to make frequent visits to Janet Montgomery on the Hudson River.

In 1828 Livingston was appointed to the United States Senate from Louisiana, and in 1831, Secretary of State. From 1833 to 1835 he served as Minister to France, living abroad for two years with Louise and Coralie and her husband, Thomas Barton, a Philadelphia Quaker. They returned to Montgomery Place in 1835, spent the summer there, and began to renovate the grounds. Edward died unexpectedly on May 23,

ABOVE *The drawing room contains furnishings collected over the generations, wallpaper untouched since its installation in the mid-19th century, and a handsome French chandelier added in the 1870s.*

LEFT *The Montgomery Place dining room opens into the drawing room through large double doors. The room contains portraits of Margaret Beekman Livingston and Chancellor Robert Livingston attributed to Gilbert Stuart. The exotic chandelier and candelabra with their morning glory detail are from Vienna and were purchased in 1856. The coats of arms of branches of the family testify to the Livingstons' love of genealogy and the esoterica of family history.*

1836. The estate was left to Louise and Coralie, and it is they who made the extensive changes we see today.

Louise Livingston and the Bartons lived in Philadelphia but spent their summers on the Hudson. During their stay abroad they may well have found the inspiration to improve their house and grounds. In 1839, the English architect Frederick Catherwood was hired to build an extraordinary Gothic Revival orangery, demolished around 1880, and in 1841 Alexander J. Davis appeared on the scene. Davis's fame as an architect had spread following the publication of his book, *Rural Residences*, in 1838. Perhaps the Donaldsons, next door at Blithewood, made the introduction. Davis had been working there since 1836, and the Livingstons must have seen the changes he had made to the house and grounds formerly owned by their uncle, General John Armstrong.

Davis worked on the house from 1841 to 1843, making additions and alterations in a highly decorative, mid-century Classical style. He added wings to the north and south, embellished with pilasters based on the Tower of the Winds in Athens. He built terraces on the east and west sides, punctuated with urns set onto pedestals. The chimneys were gathered into a new balustrade ornamented with laurel wreaths, cornices added over the windows, shutters and sash replaced, and the stucco scored and painted to imitate stone. In 1863 Davis added a curved portico, with more urns and a

frieze decorated with laurel and rosettes, all based loosely on the Temple of Vesta in Tivoli, near Rome. The overall result was delightful, and quite unique for Davis, a kind of miniaturized version of Nash's garden façade at Buckingham Palace, home at the time of the universally loved Queen Victoria.

The Bartons took a special interest in the grounds. They consulted from 1844 on with Andrew Jackson Downing, and in 1849 planned an arboretum with Hans Jacob Ehlers. Davis was directed to design numerous garden buildings, including a farmhouse and coach house, several gazebos and a bridge. Coralie Barton was a perceptive and exacting client. In asking Davis to design a small toolhouse for her husband, she wrote, "The Building ought not to be more than fourteen feet. An octagon or circle would be best adapted to the position…It would look better with steps…As the surrounding trees are very large the building ought to be lofty not to look dumpish."

Davis continued to work until 1873, when Coralie Livingston Barton died and the embellishment of Montgomery Place came to an abrupt end. Coralie's New Orleans cousins moved in, or stayed on, under the terms of a life tenancy, and Montgomery Place fell on hard times. In 1921, it passed to General John Ross Delafield, a Livingston cousin, New York lawyer, and avid collector of Livingston memorabilia. The Delafield family continued to live there until 1986, when title was conveyed to Historic Hudson Valley. The house and grounds have been open to the public since 1988.

Edgewater

OPPOSITE *French doors lead from the drawing room and dining room out to the porch of the west façade, with views of the Hudson River framed by the columns of a monumental classical portico.*

RIGHT *The guest house (top), main house (center), and pool house (bottom) form a trio of neoclassical pavilions, each facing toward the edge of the river.*

Edgewater is one of a number of houses built by the "Clermont" branch of the Livingston family, stretching all the way from Tivoli to Rhinebeck. John R. Livingston, the builder of Edgewater, was one of ten children of Judge Robert R. Livingston and his wife, Margaret Beekman, proprietors of Clermont. Judge Livingston's father inherited 13,000 acres of the original Livingston Manor in Columbia County, but Margaret Beekman brought to the marriage a dowry of 240,000 acres, her share of the famed Beekman Patent. The Livingstons connected these properties with additional purchases all along the Hudson River, and it is on these lands that Robert's and Margaret's children built their many houses.

Among these houses were Mill Hill (later called Blithewood), Montgomery Place, La Bergerie (later called Rokeby), Linwood, Grasmere, Staatsburgh, and Wildercliff. In 1797 John R. Livingston built his house just south of Montgomery Place, and named it Massena. On November 29, 1824, a deed was recorded in Dutchess County of a gift transferring 250 acres of the Massena property from John R. Livingston to his daughter Margaret and her husband, Captain Lowdnes Brown. It is said that Livingston built Edgewater as a wedding present for the young couple.

He chose a dramatic site on a small spit of land, bordered by the Hudson on three sides, and hired a mason to build a handsome brick house. He planted locust trees all around to ward off lightning, built a granite seawall to stabilize the shore, and to further protect the house from the water, set it up on a high brick basement. He hired carpenters to install the doors and windows, wide plank floors, and handsome curving staircase, and a plasterer to pull the ceiling cornices. A kitchen was built in the basement, a living room and dining room on the main floor, and bedrooms on the floors above. Finally, to give the house just the right measure of dignity, Livingston ordered up a handsome portico, with six monumental columns, carefully detailed in accordance with the rules and proportions of the Roman Doric style.

ABOVE *The drawing room contains a suite of late Federal-style Duncan Phyfe furniture including a sofa and four chairs. The portrait over the mantelpiece is of George Washington.*

RIGHT *The reception room is painted in its original red color. The sofa is by Duncan Phyfe. The harp once belonged to Mrs. Robert Donaldson.*

It is interesting to note that buildings constructed in the shape of a Greek or Roman temple were virtually unheard of in America before the Revolution and were very rare during the Federal period. Thomas Jefferson built the Virginia State Capitol in Richmond in 1789, and by the 1820s the temple form had become popular for the design of schools, churches, and banks. However, Edgewater was one of the first American houses built in the temple style, anticipating by several years the Greek Revival houses so fashionable in the 1830s.

Captain Brown was a Yale graduate, a veteran of the War of 1812, and a native of Charleston, South Carolina. As originally built, the house in some ways resembled the architecture of Charleston in the 1820s. It has been conjectured that Captain Brown influenced the design or even used a Southern architect, perhaps Robert Mills. In the same spirit, it is also interesting to note that Edgewater has a sibling, in Farmington, Connecticut, in the General Cowles House. This house, although not as handsome, shares with Edgewater the use of brick construction and sandstone trim, and a monumental colonnade set onto a high basement. Even the dormers are similar. The Cowles House has also reminded visitors of the South, and one wrote in 1926 "...the whole thing looks well, and quite like Charleston." It is fanciful to imagine that General Cowles and Captain Brown may have met during their military service, or at Yale, and possibly shared the same builder.

The Browns enjoyed the use of their house for many years until Captain Brown died in 1851. At the same time the Hudson River Railroad arrived, and by power of eminent domain cut the property in two. Railroad tracks appeared fifty feet to the east of the front door. In anger and frustration, Margaret Livingston decided to sell and found a willing buyer in Robert Donaldson. The deed, dated February 3, 1853, recorded the price at $22,500.

ABOVE *The gracious Federal-style staircase leads from the entrance hall to the second floor.*

RIGHT *The master bedroom contains a handsome canopied four-poster bed, with southwestern views of the Hudson River beyond.*

OPPOSITE *The dining room is furnished with a suite of Duncan Phyfe chairs and French porcelain which once belonged to the Livingston family.*

Donaldson was a native of North Carolina who traveled to London as a young man of twenty-one to claim an uncle's legacy of $300,000 and returned to New York to set himself up in business. He was something of an aesthete and patron of the arts, counting among his friends Washington Irving, Asher Durand, and Samuel F. B. Morse. Charles R. Leslie painted his portrait and Andrew Downing dedicated a book to him, calling him an "Arbiter Elegantiarum." Donaldson commissioned architect Alexander J. Davis to make some changes to his New York townhouse and remained loyal to Davis for the rest of his life. After Donaldson retired in 1837, he and Davis spent the next fifteen years turning General John Armstrong's old property at Annandale into a gentleman's farm, bracketed gate lodge and all, renaming it Blithewood. In 1852 he sold Blithewood to John Bard and invited Davis up for a "final ramble." His reasons were clear. He had sold to Bard for $500 an acre and bought from Margaret Brown for $90 an acre. He wrote to Davis that he had bought the new property as a "speculation."

Donaldson intended to commission Davis to build a house to the east, up on the hill, a site with a better view, and then sub-

OPPOSITE LEFT AND BELOW *Views of a neo-classical guest house, completed in 1998. The pedimental entablature and Doric columns make reference to the architectural details of the main house. A monumental staircase leads to the river's edge.*

BELOW *The classically detailed poolhouse makes an elegant backdrop for the new swimming pool.*

divide the property with additional houses to be sold. In the meantime, he moved into Mrs. Brown's house and soon changed his mind, writing to Davis: "You will be surprised (perhaps grieved) to learn that I have given up all purposes of Building a Villa upon the Heights & intend to live & die in this Greek Temple!"

Surely Davis was grieved. But soon Donaldson asked him to design a new library addition at the north side of the house, a bay window to the south, and requested designs for "a Green House, a Prospect Tower & Observatory on the Little Island—a Boat House, Gate, Sabbath School House, etc." In 1854, based on Davis's designs, Donaldson built the octagonal library and in 1855, with Davis's help, stuccoed, scored and marbleized the brick walls of the house, adding, for good measure, a grass terrace to the west lawn to hide the basement wall. These alterations transformed the neo-classical temple into a picturesque villa and gave it its decidedly romantic character.

It was Donaldson who changed the name of the estate from Sylvania, first to River Lawn, and then to Edgewater.

Donaldson died in 1872, and a long period of decline ensued. In 1902 his heirs sold the property to Elizabeth Chanler and her husband, the writer John Jay Chapman. Elizabeth Chanler grew up at Rokeby, just to the south, and was a great-granddaughter of General John Armstrong and Alida Livingston. Thus, the property returned once more to the Livingston family. In 1904, the Chapmans commissioned the architect Charles Adams Platt to build a new house and garden on the hill above Edgewater, to be called by the old name "Sylvania," and in 1917 sold Edgewater to their son, Conrad.

Gore Vidal, the writer, bought the house in 1950 and lived there in Bohemian splendor at a time when the Red Hook area had become something of a literary colony. He wrote books, involved himself in local politics, built a swimming pool and invited his many friends to visit, including Alice Astor, Eleanor Roosevelt, Paul Newman, and Joanne Woodward. It is said that he adapted to the sound of the railroad with characteristic wit, indulging himself at the dinner table in long anecdotes, and then turning to a guest to say (just before the train's noisy arrival), "now tell me about your life." In 1969 he sold the house and moved to Amalfi on the Tyrrhenian coast, by which time Edgewater was falling apart and left with only two-and-a-half of its original 250 acres.

Like Robert Donaldson, the new owner, Richard H. Jenrette, is a native of North Carolina and a New York financier. He has restored the house to the spirit of the Donaldson years, refreshingly free of the rules and regulations of historic preservation. He has retrieved many of the furnishings of the Livingston and Donaldson families, seeming to command them over time to return to Edgewater. In recent years, he bought back much of the original acreage and created a kind of *jardin anglaise*, complete with landscaped meadow, entrance court with parterres and obelisks, and two new neoclassical garden buildings.

Wilderstein

Robert Livingston, the first Lord of the Manor of Livingston, had three sons who survived him: Philip, who became the second Lord of the Manor; Robert, who received 13,000 acres of the Manor, on which he built Clermont; and Gilbert, the least-favored son, who was left some land in Saratoga, but no part of the Manor. Gilbert married Cornelia Beekman, the daughter of Henry Beekman, the patentee of thousands of acres near Rhinebeck. They had fourteen children, one of whom, Alida Livingston, was the grandmother of Catherine Rutsen, the second wife of George Suckley.

George Suckley was an Englishman who came to Baltimore in the 1780s as the representative of a hardware company. He had much greater ambitions and began to invest in real estate in New York. After the death of his first wife, he married Catherine Rutsen and in this way connected himself to the Beekman family. With the help of this connection and his own efforts, Suckley grew rich. He invested in more land, in mining and steamships, and founded the Greenwich Savings Bank.

He died in 1846 and left his business to his sons, Rutsen and Thomas, both of whom managed their assets wisely. In 1852 in order to have a house in the country near his Beekman cousins, Thomas Suckley bought thirty-two acres that belonged to Wildercliff, an estate owned by the Garretsons, a branch of the Clermont Livingstons who were, like the Suckleys, staunchly Methodist. Thomas Suckley called on John Warren Ritch, an architect who rented space in one of Suckley's New York buildings, and bought from him drawings for a modest, two-story Italianate villa, probably adapted from one of the designs Suckley had seen in Ritch's book, *The American Architect*. For the next thirty-six years, until his death in 1888, Suckley enjoyed life with his family at this house overlooking the Hudson River.

When Thomas Suckley died, all of the wealth accumulated over two generations was left to Robert Bowne Suckley, his only surviving child. Robert Suckley was born in 1856, four years after his father built his house, studied law and married Elizabeth Montgomery, another Livingston who lived in New York City. Suckley chose not to work but to live on the interest from his investments. He described his occupation as "gentleman," and with his fortune secure, set about to embellish and enlarge Wilderstein. Nearly all of the changes he made survive today.

Suckley hired Arnout Cannon, Jr., a Poughkeepsie architect, to design the alterations and a new carriage house as well. Cannon added a third floor, a servants' wing and a five-story tower, and specified a polychromatic color scheme of mauve, pumpkin, tan and green, all in the Queen Anne style. Suckley loved gadgets. He was fasci-

From the wrap-around verandah with its cooling breezes the family delighted in the magnificent views of river and landscape. A favorite gathering place, it continues to be enjoyed as an outside living room from early spring through the fall. The views and paths of the landscape designed by Calvert Vaux in 1891 are being reclaimed today. Trees and shrubs planted by him and still in existence include redbuds, ginkgos, fringe trees, hydrangeas, spirea, mock orange, and jet bead. Trails with picturesque viewing sites and rustic gazebos cross Wilderstein's forty acres.

nated by the automobile and by 1910 owned five of them. In his house, he installed burglar alarms, a servants' call system, a telephone and a large number of electric clocks. He held the franchise for electricity in Orange, New Jersey, and had Wilderstein electrified, an improvement made possible by the construction of a hydroelectric generator on the Landsman's Kill.

In 1889 Suckley commissioned Joseph Burr Tiffany to fit out the five principal rooms on the first floor. These improvements included a paneled dining room, with stained glass windows embellished with the armorial crests of the Chew, Livingston, Tillotson, and Lynch families, and the newly created Suckley coat of arms. Tiffany installed a new oak staircase, a Gothic Revival library, and a parlor done up in the style of Louis XVI, with a ceiling canvas by H. Siddons Mowbray. In 1890 not content with these alterations, Suckley hired Calvert Vaux to create a landscape plan. Vaux, the one-time protégé of Downing and former partner of Frederick Law Olmsted, was now an old man. Wilderstein was his last private commission before he wandered into Gravesend Bay one night in 1895 and drowned.

For its time and place, Wilderstein was a modest house, created for a rather eccentric family of independent means, in sharp contrast to the alterations at Staatsburg and Hyde Park, where the funds and ambitions were limitless. Wilderstein's Queen Anne architecture was soon out of fashion. Suckley inherited Wilderstein four years before the World's Columbian Exposition, held in Chicago in 1892-93, where the great white pavilions signaled the end of 19th-century "styles," and the beginning of the revival of the classicism used to great effect on behalf of the Mills and Vanderbilt families.

Like the style of his house, Suckley's investments suffered with time. For a while he moved his wife and six children to Switzerland, to conserve his diminished resources. When Robert Suckley died in 1921, he left Wilderstein to a wife and grown

children who were constrained by the expense of its upkeep, and unprepared to earn the money to pay for it. His eldest daughter, Margaret Suckley, became a paid companion to her mother's sister in New York City to help meet the family finances.

Franklin Delano Roosevelt was a distant cousin of the Suckleys. He returned to Hyde Park, on account of his bout with polio, and renewed his acquaintance with the Suckley family. Margaret Suckley became his close companion, and it was she who gave FDR his famous Scottie dog, Fala. She helped him with the design of his hideaway, Top Cottage, and was among those with him when he died at Warm Springs, Georgia. She was appointed Assistant Archivist at the FDR Library when it opened and remained there for over twenty years. Margaret Suckley was the last of her family, and in 1983 she gave the house and grounds to Wilderstein Preservation, a group of volunteers. She died at Wilderstein, in 1991, in the same house where she had been born nearly one hundred years earlier.

The griffin motif, part of the Montgomery coat of arms depicted in the entrance hall andirons and newel post shown on pages 84-85, is repeated in the overmantel of the dining room fireplace. Two griffins flank a shield in carved mahogany. A pair of American Art pottery vases ornamented with pink and white blossoms and green leaves adorn the mantel. The boxed beamed ceiling provides a rich matrix of mahogany carving and millwork. The walls are mahogany panels below a band of wool tapestry in a golden chrysanthemum design and surmounted by a plaster frieze painted to resemble mahogany. The walls, which echo the arrangement in the entrance hall, feature oak panels below a band of tooled leather surmounted by a plaster frieze painted silver.

OPPOSITE TOP
The siting of the house at an angle to the river was done on purpose so that, when the trees were cut away, one could look straight down the Hudson River (see page 81). Just visible through the cutting is "Umbrella Point" from which, on a clear day, one can see the Shawangunk Mountains.

OPPOSITE BOTTOM
Designed by Arnout Cannon in 1888 as part of the expansion of the site, the Carriage House with its onion dome and fanciful ventilators awaits restoration and adaptive reuse.

Perhaps because Robert Suckley's descendants lacked the means to make changes to Wilderstein, and because they held so tenaciously onto what was already built, the estate is one of the most well-preserved Hudson River estates to survive. The Suckleys saved everything, including records of their family dating back to the early 18th century, records of their business ventures, 20,000 photographs, architectural drawings, landscape plans, books, art, furniture, textiles, costumes, and the bric-a-brac of daily life. The unspoiled condition of Wilderstein and its furnishings, and the intact state of its voluminous archives, record an important part of the social and architectural history of the Hudson River Valley and of a family that once lived there.

Staatsburgh

aptain Henry Pawling was an officer in the English army which came to New Netherland when the English replaced the Dutch in 1664. He bought 4,000 acres of land in Dutchess County from the Indians, a title confirmed by Crown Patent in 1698. In 1701 his family sold a portion of this land to Dr. Samuel Staats, who gave his name to the surrounding neighborhood.

In time, Dr. Staats's land passed down to his granddaughter Sarah Gouveneur and her husband, Lewis Morris, a signer of the Declaration of Independence and the proprietor of the Manor of Morrisania in the Bronx. In 1792 they sold the land to Morgan and Gertrude Lewis who, sometime around 1795, built a brick house overlooking the Hudson, and named it Staatsburgh. Morgan Lewis was the son of Francis Lewis, a Welsh-man who came to New York, succeeded in business and politics and also signed the Declaration of Independence. Morgan graduated from Princeton in 1773, studied law, served in the American Revolution under General Gates and became the third governor of New York. In 1779 he married Gertrude Livingston, one of the children of Robert and Margaret Livingston of Clermont, the same children who built the

Guests entered the house through the main hall which, like the exterior and the surrounding grounds, was intended to have an English feeling. Oak paneling in the Baroque style of the late 17th and early 18th centuries served as a backdrop for rich tapestries and the row of ancestral portraits that reminded guests of Mrs. Mills's distinguished lineage. The two primary architectural features of the room are the grand staircase and the fireplace. Both are larger than necessary but deliberately designed to impress. Suspended over the grand staircase is an illusionistic painting on the ceiling that gives the appearance of opening directly onto a sky filled with mythological figures.

The dining room, located in one of the new wings, is designed in the French Baroque style of Louis XIV and much more exuberant than the English Baroque style of the main hall. The large stately room expresses a feeling of power. Much of the spectacular quality of the room is derived from the abundant use of costly materials—marble on the walls and floor, early 18th century Flemish tapestries, immense mirrors and sheets of window glass, an oversized Turkish carpet and the expansive use of gold.

long row of houses along the Hudson from Clermont four miles south to Staatsburgh.

Staatsburgh as originally built was two stories high, rectangular in shape, with brick walls. In this regard it was similar to other houses in the vicinity, of the Federal period, such as Mazefield, Rokeby, and Linwood. Morgan and Gertrude Lewis lived there with their daughter Margaret, her husband, Maturin Livingston, and their twelve grandchildren. One granddaughter called it a "capacious brick house—as ugly as it was comfortable" noting that it was built on top of one of the best sledding hills in the neighborhood. In 1832 it burned while the family was in New York. A photograph of the house, as rebuilt, suggests the possibility that the builders reused the masonry walls of the original house but added new porches to the east and west façades, supported by large Greek columns that were designed, according to the family legend, by Margaret Lewis Livingston. During its time as a private house, Staatsburgh belonged to only one family, and over time Morgan and Gertrude Lewis's house became the property of their great-granddaughter, Ruth Livingston Mills.

Ruth Livingston was a Van Rensselaer on her mother's side and one of the sixth generation of Livingstons descended from the first Lord of the Manor, Robert Livingston. It is safe to say that she came from an old family. By this time most of the Livingstons were removed from the social arena and preferred to socialize among themselves on the tennis courts of the Edgewood Club at Tivoli. They must have

RIGHT *The library, in the other of the two wings added to the mansion during the 1895 remodeling, has the same dimensions as the dining room. Like the dining room, its walls and ceilings are in the Louis XIV style. The walls are paneled in quarter-sawn oak. The architecture of the room is enhanced by various decorative trophies: instruments associated with the exploration and control of land—globes, charts, torches, telescopes, and compasses; heads representing land and sea; and stylized, allegorical symbols of America. While these elements might not seem to be consistent with a Louis XIV room, they were deliberately selected to communicate the family's heritage in the formation of America.*

ABOVE *The entertaining spaces were arranged enfilade on the west side of the house. Peering from the windows, guests could enjoy views of the sloping lawns dotted with specimen trees, the distant Catskills, and the sun setting over the Hudson River.*

The sitting room was used by Mrs. Mills and lady guests as a place in which quiet conversation could be conducted. Mrs. Mills would also meet here with senior household staff to attend to all the responsibilities that came with the management of the large household. The ivory-colored walls are embellished with gold leaf.

been at least mildly surprised when, in 1882, Ruth Livingston married Ogden Mills, the son of Darius Mills and the heir to a California Gold Rush fortune worth upwards of $60 million. Their marriage united a member of the Hudson Valley's landed, but financially diminished, gentry with the heir to a great deal of new money, money that allowed Ruth Livingston Mills to embark on an ambitious social program and to embellish her modest, twenty-five room ancestral home.

She inherited Staatsburgh in 1890, and three years later hired the New York architects McKim, Mead & White, possibly at the suggestion of Whitelaw Reid, Ogden Mills's brother-in-law and a client of the firm. The partner-in-charge, Stanford White, added two floors to the original house and concealed them under a monumental entrance porch. He built new wings to the north and south, both somewhat larger than

The drawing room is located in the center core of the house, which dates back to 1832. It was then two rooms. During the 1895 remodeling the wall was removed in order to create one, larger, room. It was to this room that ladies "withdrew" after dinner while gentlemen remained at the dining room table to continue conversations considered indelicate for women.

the original house, and decorated the façades with fluted ionic pilasters and a bracketed cornice, all in the manner of the Englishman James Gibbs, 18th-century architect of large country houses. Staatsburgh bears a striking resemblance to the design of the White House, designed by William Hoban, but also derived from the work of Gibbs.

Ruth and Ogden Mills used Staatsburgh in the fall, when they were not at their houses in New York, Newport, California, or Paris. Guests came for house parties and to join in the legendary bridge games. When not playing cards, the guests could entertain themselves with golf, tennis, or riding horseback.

Staatsburgh eventually became the property of the Mills' son, Ogden Livingston Mills, who was Secretary of the Treasury during the Hoover administration, and later his sister, Gladys Mills Phipps. In 1938 Mrs. Phipps gave the house and 192 acres to the State of New York as a memorial to her parents, and in 1970 added the contents of the house to her gift. Today the property is operated by the New York State Office of Parks, Recreation and Historic Preservation and is open to the public.

Hyde Park
The Vanderbilt Mansion

"Hyde Park is justly celebrated as one of the finest specimens of the Romantic style of landscape gardening in America."
Andrew Jackson Downing, 1841.

The mansion of Frederick and Louise Vanderbilt at Hyde Park occupies the same striking site as the house of the estate's former owner, Walter Langdon, and that of the owner before him. McKim, Mead & White designed, constructed, and decorated this Beaux-Arts mansion between 1895 and 1899. It became the centerpiece for an approximately 675-acre country estate comprised of park and farm land on the eastern shore of the Hudson River. Of particular appeal to the Vanderbilts, the estate had an unparalleled view of the river and the Catskill mountains to the west, and already boasted an aged collection of specimen trees, a superbly designed Parmentier landscape over 100 years old, and a substantial farm operation. While the Vanderbilts purchased and sold other homes over the remaining years of their lives, Hyde Park seemingly remained a continuing source of pleasure to them.

Frederick William Vanderbilt, who built the house at Hyde Park, was the grandson of Cornelius Vanderbilt. Cornelius built a fortune in shipping and railroads worth over $100 million at his death, having gone to work at the age of eleven on his father's ferryboat. He left most of it to his son, William Henry Vanderbilt, at a time when there was no estate tax. When the son died in 1885, his eight children, including Frederick, placed a portion of their inheritance in the service of architecture and built a series of great houses, both on Fifth Avenue, and throughout the country at fashionable places where the wealthy congregated.

Frederick Vanderbilt was the third son and inherited about $10 million, a modest share compared to his elder brothers, who received about $100 million each. Vanderbilt graduated from the Sheffield School of Engineering at Yale University, and in 1878 married Louise Holmes Anthony. He was a shy and retiring man with a passion for yachting who belonged to numerous yacht clubs and built *Rainbow*, the America's Cup defender in 1934. By contrast, his wife was outgoing and eccentric, a Christian Scientist with an interest in astrology and a passion for biographies of Marie Antoinette and Josephine Bonaparte.

Frederick and Louise Vanderbilt lived in the style to which the wealthy were accustomed during the Gilded Age. They maintained houses in New York, Newport, Bar Harbor and Palm Beach. They lived at Hyde Park in April and May, and again in the fall until Thanksgiving. The house, the grounds and the elegant, well-decorated rooms were a magnificent playhouse where they and their friends entertained themselves during an endless series of weekend house parties. Behind the scenes was a staff of sixty-two, including butlers, chambermaids, cooks and parlor maids.

Hyde Park had a long history before the Vanderbilts arrived in 1895. In 1772, Dr. John Bard, a well-known New York physician, retired there and lived at Red House, on the east side of the Albany Post Road. In 1795, his son, Dr. Samuel Bard, built a large house and garden on the plateau overlooking the Hudson River, where he lived until his death in 1821. The property was sold in 1828 to Dr. David Hosack, a student of Samuel Bard and later his partner.

ABOVE *Flanking the elliptical hall, the den is a warm and intimate space connected to Mr. Vanderbilt's private office through a bathroom. Designed by Georges Glaenzer, a French èmigrè decorator, the room includes a number of Renaissance-style elements. The walls are paneled in Santo Domingo mahogany and the ceiling contains elaborately carved panels. The ceiling is ornamented with encased cross-timbers around a large carved central medallion. The upper portions of the west wall contain curved arches with faux finishes replicating tapestries and carved wood. The large fireplace mantel is decorated with a Staffordshire clock and pair of candelabra, a wedding gift from Mr. Vanderbilt's father. The east wall bookcases contain large sets of bound literature, while those on the west wall are filled with less formal and seemingly more personal collections. The room is furnished with upholstered sofas, easy chairs, a library table and eclectic accessories, including several mounted animal heads. The Vanderbilts used it as a family living room when they came alone to Hyde Park or when entertaining their closest family and friends.*

RIGHT *The elliptical entrance hall was designed in the French Renaissance style by Charles McKim. Entering the structure's main east doorway, guests face wide French doors to the west portico flanking a broad fireplace. To left and right, wide symmetrical foyers lead to the living and dining rooms. Overhead, a decorated octagonal light well reveals a double row of stone balusters on the second floor, and over that, an octagonal skylight. The lightwell design was changed substantially from McKim's original opening when the Vanderbilts requested the firm of Warren and Wetmore to redesign the second floor hall and the living room in 1906. The entrance hall furnishings include pieces brought from the Vanderbilt's New York City townhouse and pieces purchased by Stanford White in Europe, among them the marble mantel, the pair of reproduction Louis XIV busts, and the antique and composite cabinets that flank the front door. A 17th-century tapestry depicting the Medici coat of arms hangs over the fireplace. Historically, the room was decorated with numerous oriental and animal skin rugs and antique tapestry portieres no longer in place. Guests could relax here before the fire in the literal center of the house.*

Hosack was a physician and a professor of medicine and botany at Columbia. He was the attending physician at the duel between Aaron Burr and Alexander Hamilton, and in 1801, he founded the Elgin Botanical Garden, the first public botanical garden in the United States, on the site of what is now Rockefeller Center. Making use of the fortune of his third wife, Magdalene Coster, Hosack built a Greek Revival house at Hyde Park and engaged the services of André Parmentier, a well-known Belgian land-scape designer. Parmentier prepared plans for a picturesque park with winding roads, walking paths and gardens, all of which formed the landscape that is largely intact today. Parmentier's design, common at the time in Europe, was unprecedented in America, and the park became a mecca for visitors. Among them was Andrew Jackson

OPPOSITE *The living room occupies the entire south end of the house and is identical in size to the dining room on the north end. Designed by Charles McKim, the walls are paneled in Circassian walnut. The two large marble mantelpieces on the south wall balance the pair in the dining room. The ceiling is divided into panels with elaborate molded borders and originally contained paintings by muralist H. Siddons Mowbray, removed in the 1906 renovation. The walls are decorated with large tapestries—one pair with Medici family coat of arms, and another pair from a set of four by Martin Rambeaux illustrating scenes from the Trojan War (the remaining two hang in the foyer outside the living room). Stanford White purchased the French silk velvet for the draperies, the large rug in the center of the room, several tables, and the twisted black marble columns flanking the French doors to the south portico. Furniture includes a number of Louis XV-style sofas and armchairs, large refectory tables—probably combining antique and modern elements— and 19th-century reproductions of an elaborate French desk and tables by the celebrated French cabinetmaker Paul Sormani. The 1880 Steinway grand piano is one of the few American-made pieces in the house. It was brought to Hyde Park from the Vanderbilt's 5th Avenue townhouse in New York City. Originally clear-finished rosewood veneer, the Vanderbilts had the case gilded and decorated with floral designs, landscape scenes, and the portraits of classical composers. The decoration is typical of other "art case" Steinways from the period, and may have been commissioned when the piano was purchased.*

RIGHT *The formal Renaissance style dining room is paneled in dark walnut with carved, gilded borders. After the decoration was in place, the Vanderbilts requested that the gilding be toned down—probably to give the room an appearance of age. The entrance is flanked by two Cippolini marble columns, balancing a pair in the living room. The elaborate 17th-century coffered ceiling, decorated with gilding and recessed painted panels, was imported from Italy by Stanford White. Herter Brothers, a once-prominent New York decorating firm, expanded the ceiling to fit the required room size. The central panel frames a mural painted by Edward Simmons. The north wall supports two massive antique stone fireplaces from France and Italy. The room is also decorated with a pair of gilded antique Florentine mirrors, and a pair of antique English planetaria. A fine old Isphahan carpet measuring 20' x 40' and selected by Stanford White, occupies the center of the room. The large table seats eighteen guests and was decorated with as many as two thousand roses from the estate's extensive greenhouses. The small round table was used for breakfast and when the Vanderbilts dined alone.*

Downing, who became the leading theorist of landscape design of the Hudson River Valley, if not the nation. Downing, of necessity self-taught, mainly from the books written by English designers, was understandably impressed by his first visit to a landscape created in the Romantic style he so admired.

In 1840, John Jacob Astor bought the house and 108 acres as a gift for his daughter Dorothea, who was known as Dolly. On a trip to Washington, Dolly Astor met a dashing but poor New Englander named Colonel Walter Langdon, with whom she eloped, and Astor vowed never to forgive them. It is said that seven years later Astor went to a children's party at the house of a friend, met a pretty six year old and asked her name. When she replied, "my name is Sarah Sherburne Langdon," Astor declared, "For your sake, I shall have to forgive your mother and father." The house that Astor bought burned down in 1845, Walter Langdon built another, and it was this house that stood on the site when Frederick Vanderbilt bought Hyde Park in 1895.

Vanderbilt hired McKim, Mead & White, the New York architecture firm that had already built two houses for Frederick Vanderbilt's sisters. They were directed to renovate and expand the existing house, as they had done for Ogden Mills at nearby

OPPOSITE *Mrs. Vanderbilt's suite was designed in the Louis XV style by Ogden Codman—the author, with Edith Wharton, of* The Decoration of Houses, *published during his work on this Vanderbilt commission. Codman was especially well-known for his adaptations of 18th-century French styles. This bedchamber is designed in the manner of a French State chamber, with a curved railing separating the bed from the room at large. The doorway to Mr. Vanderbilt's suite was moved during the design, and an additional blank door was designed to line up with the room's east windows and ensure the required symmetry of the room. The walls were painted gray with gilt-bordered panels, as was her boudoir (above) and inset with copies of paintings by Charles Josef Natoire and Francois Boucher in the Hotel Soubise, Paris. The original paintings selected by Codman were replaced at Mrs. Vanderbilt's request, probably in 1913. Also in 1913, the Vanderbilts replaced the original rug with the Savonnerie carpet now in place. The walls surrounding the bed are covered in a fine silk fabric, and the draperies and bed hangings are constructed of elaborately embroidered green silk. Codman designed a number of the furnishings for the room including the bed, a pair of armchairs, and a chaise longue. A pair of reproduction 18th-century commodes decorated with ormolu and a vitrine table were made by French cabinet-maker Paul Sormani. Even by Vanderbilt standards, this was an extravagant and pretentious space. Codman's exquisite drawings of the room are part of the site collections.*

ABOVE *Mrs. Vanderbilt's Boudoir. The room's original paintings were replaced by the Vanderbilts, probably when her bedroom paintings were changed. The lavish Louis XV style furnishings include a dressing table, day bed, a painted screen, a number of caned chairs and a settee. The draperies are finely embroidered cream silk. A tall closet could be accessed by servants from the second floor hall without disturbing Mrs. Vanderbilt. The room has two additional closets, one containing a jewelry safe.*

Staatsburgh, but this proved impossible when serious problems were discovered in the wood-frame structure. The architects prepared a new design, along the lines of the original house, but greatly refined, framed in steel instead of wood, and clad in Indiana limestone in place of the original stucco. The Lodge was built first (in an amazing sixty-six days) so that the Vanderbilts could live at Hyde Park while their new house was under construction. The shell of the house, the work of Charles McKim, was finished in 1898, but the fit-out of the interior, built to designs by McKim's partner, Stanford White, Ogden Codman, Jr., and George Glaenzer, took another year to complete.

OPPOSITE Mr. Vanderbilt's bedchamber occupies the southwest corner of the second floor, and is entered from the foyer at the south end. A concealed doorway provides access to Mrs. Vanderbilt's adjoining suite. Georges Glaenzer elaborately decorated this princely room with bold, masculine features, including upholstered walls with over 700 square feet of 17th-century tapestries. The dark walnut paneling is decorated with high relief grotesque faces and terminates toward a ceiling constructed of elaborately molded plaster with carved cross-members and large central medallion. A pair of monumental twisted columns with gilded decoration frame the bed. The ornately carved Renaissance chimney-breast is decorated with a pair of classical warriors. The Indian rugs, the velvet draperies and upholstery, and historically, the flower arrangements, reflect Mr. Vanderbilt's preference for the color red.

TOP RIGHT The Pavilion was built in1895 as a temporary residence for the Vanderbilts who wanted to be close to the construction of the new mansion. Originally they were going to use an existing structure but it was found to be unsafe and so the present one was constructed. It was completed in an extraordinary sixty-six working days, with men working shoulder to shoulder. Later it was used as housing for the Vanderbilts' bachelor guests, where they would retire after dinner for billiards, cigars, and brandy. The classical Greek-style structure is finished in pebble dash, and historically was painted yellow with white trim. Following the estate's transfer to the National Park Service in 1940, the building briefly served as a tea room and inn. Today it serves as a Visitor Center and exhibit space for orienting the public to the site.

BOTTOM RIGHT The coach house was designed by Robert Henderson Robertson in about 1898. Robertson had previously designed a string of railroad stations along Frederick Vanderbilt's Hudson River line. At the same time, Robertson was also designing Shelburne Farms, Shelburne, Vermont, for Mr. Vanderbilt's sister and brother-in-law, Lila Vanderbilt Webb and Seward Webb. The Queen Anne-style structure was typical for turn-of-the-century carriage houses and stables. The structure was renovated to accommodate motor vehicles shortly after, but continued to serve as a stable and carriage barn for recreational riding and coaching. Today the structure continues to house a collection of carriages and automobiles, including Mr. Vanderbilt's 1933 16-cylinder Cadillac.

Mckim, Mead & White designed several garden buildings, including the gate lodges, and Robert Henderson Robertson, another favorite of the Vanderbilt family, designed the stables. James Leal Greenleaf, a landscape designer, made substantial

changes to the formal gardens built by the Langdons, replaced the greenhouses, and developed the Parmentier landscape.

Louise Vanderbilt died in Paris in 1926. By the time Frederick Vanderbilt died in 1938 their way of life was a thing of the past, brought to an end by vast social change, the Great Depression and the estate tax. Vanderbilt had managed his fortune well and left an estate valued at $78 million. However, of this, inheritance taxes claimed fifty percent, and most of the rest went to Vanderbilt University, Frederick's alma mater Yale University, and the medical hospital at Columbia. Vanderbilt left bequests of up to $250,000 to employees who had faithfully served him at Hyde Park during his thirty-nine years of ownership. This was not as unusual as it might seem, for Frederick and Louise had long been known for their generosity toward the servants, paid them well, provided them medical insurance, and college tuition for their children.

The Vanderbilts had no children, and Margaret Louise Van Alen, a favorite niece of Mrs. Vanderbilt, inherited all of Frederick's private property. Well established in Newport, Mrs. Van Alen placed Hyde Park on the market soon after her uncle's death. The initial asking price of $350,000 was subsequently lowered to $250.000—

very little considering the house alone had cost $600,000 to build in 1895. Few at the time were able to live like the Vanderbilts, and the place went unsold until President Franklin Roosevelt approached Mrs. Van Alen with the suggestion that she donate the property to the people of the United States. The National Park Service took over 211 acres of the property and opened Hyde Park to the public in 1940.

Today Hyde Park is one of the most intact houses and landscapes to remain from the Gilded Age, and allows visitors a glimpse of how the rich lived a century earlier. Operated as The Vanderbilt Mansion National Historic Site, the site symbolizes America's new role after the Civil War as a social, political, and economic force in the world, and illustrates the unprecedented wealth that came with it, and a disparity that was once understood as inappropriate to the ideals of the American republic.

The FDR Library & Museum and Homes of Franklin and Eleanor Roosevelt:
Springwood, Val-Kill, and Top Cottage

Franklin D. Roosevelt, elected four times as President of the United States, was one of the most important world leaders of the 20th century. Springwood, his ancestral home, stands eighty miles north of New York City, in Hyde Park, amid the rolling fields and wooded hills that lie above the eastern bank of the Hudson River. Roosevelt's father, James Roosevelt, moved there from Poughkeepsie with his first wife, Rebecca Howland, when they bought the Springwood property in 1867, and from that year until 1945, when Franklin Roosevelt died, Springwood remained the focal point of the Roosevelt family.

Ten years after the family moved to Springwood, Rebecca Howland died and

LEFT *The ship's bell framed in the arch was one in FDR's naval ordnance collection. It had belonged to a Spanish ship, "Isla de Cuba," and had been pulled from the water in Manila Harbor in 1898 during the Spanish-American War.*

ABOVE *The entrance hall to Springwood, leading to the living room (left) and the Dresden room (ahead). The large ornate Italian credenza was bought by Rebecca and James Roosevelt in the 1860s. Above the credenza hang naval prints of the War of 1812 from FDR's collection of sailing and naval prints, many more examples of which hang in the house. To the right of the credenza is a Sgabello chair. The grandfather clock at right was sent from Holland by James and Sara on their honeymoon.*

James Roosevelt married Sara Delano, a much younger woman. Franklin Delano Roosevelt was their only child. He was born in Springwood in 1882 and grew up riding horseback with his father and hunting specimens for his collection of stuffed birds in the meadows and forests surrounding the house. He became an expert ornithologist and learned the names of all the trees. As an adult he developed a keen interest and expertise in forestry and planted thousands of trees on abandoned farm land that he bought adjacent to Springwood. He had a detailed knowledge of local history and took a special delight in the Dutch Colonial stone architecture of the Hudson Valley. These interests shaped the evolution of the Roosevelt estate and the buildings upon it. They also influenced his policies as Governor of New York and President, especially the establishment of conservation programs such as the Civilian Conservation Corps. His deep attachment to Hyde Park and his experiences there as naturalist, tree farmer, and builder helped create the leader he became.

The living room was FDR's crowning achievement in the design of the enlarged house. The room, 30 ft x 50 ft, was designed to resemble the libraries of the "big houses" he visited in England. He particularly loved the dark wood panels with the carved elements, the large bookshelves. He left space at the top for his collection of Naval paintings and prints and Chinese porcelains collected from his mother's family, the Delanos, who were in the China 'tea' trade. The desk at the left, in the Northeast corner was his stamp desk. He spent many hours studying his collection of stamps, tuning out the bad news during the war years. He would spend an hour or so each evening getting respite from the war. His knowledge of geography knew no bounds, even impressing admirals and generals during WWII, knowing some obscure island or location particularly hit by the war.

James Roosevelt died in 1900 and Franklin Roosevelt, who had been educated at home by his doting mother, was sent to Groton Preparatory Academy. After Groton, he went to Harvard, studied law at Columbia, married Eleanor Roosevelt, his fifth cousin, and in 1910 began a career in politics with his election to the State Senate.

The Roosevelts lived with Franklin Roosevelt's mother at the townhouse they shared in New York, and in the country at Springwood. In 1915 FDR and his mother commissioned the architect Francis L.V. Hoppin to make extensive alterations, including new fieldstone wings on the north and south ends of the house. In the years to come, the handsome new Federal revival façade served as a backdrop for election night rallies.

In 1921 Roosevelt's political future was threatened when he contracted polio, but with the aid of his wife, he resumed his career and in 1928 was elected Governor of New York. He was elected President in 1932, leading the nation through the Great Depression and World War II, until his death in 1945. In 1938 toward the end of his second term as President, Roosevelt built a private retreat on a hill near the back of his Hyde Park property which by then included over 1200 acres. He called it Top

ABOVE *The Dresden room, so named for the chandelier that hangs in the center was Sara Delano Roosevelt's sitting room. In 1939 she had the room reupholstered in the Chintz florals to celebrate the visit of King George VI and Queen Elizabeth, the Queen Mother. The royal couple rarely stayed in a private house, much less the home of the President of the United States. Through the Dresden room one can see into the dining room. The chair at the head of the table was FDR's. It was always turned at an angle like this to allow him ease of access from his wheelchair.*

RIGHT *FDR and ER's master bedroom from 1915-1921. In 1921 ER moved to her dressing room east of the master bedroom as FDR needed privacy after his devastating attack of polio. He liked to lie in bed and look down the river to the South at the view. One of the wheelchairs he used in the Roosevelt home sits in the room. Designed by FDR it was actually a kitchen chair with the legs cut off and wheels placed front and back. He did not remain long on the chair but would move to a chair or couch to be more comfortable.*

ABOVE AND RIGHT Top Cottage was designed by FDR and built from local fieldstone. He made Top Cottage easily accessible to him in his wheelchair. The entrance is level with the ground, there are no threshold barriers between the doors, and there is a ramp off the large west porch. Other features, such as the low window sills, absence of a dining room, design of the bathroom, and the arrangement of the bedrooms may also reflect his needs as a wheelchair user. It is one of the earliest homes designed to be accessible to a person with a disability. FDR often came here with his cousin and friend Daisy Suckley to enjoy the quiet and the view. He brought distinguished visitors to the cottage, including King George VI of England and Queen Elizabeth (now the Queen Mother) who were entertained on the porch at the famous "hot dog" picnic. One of only two known photographs of FDR in a wheelchair was taken of him on this porch. When FDR had Top Cottage built, it is said that his mother was so upset that she made him promise never to sleep there until after she was dead. She died in 1941 but FDR never slept there, as far as we know.

Cottage and intended to use it as a quiet place to get away from the busy life of Springwood and the many people who made demands on his time. Henry Toombs, the Atlanta architect who had designed the Little White House in Warm Springs, Georgia, drew the elevations for the building, but FDR designed it and the plans were signed, "Franklin D. Roosevelt, Architect." He designed Top Cottage in the style of the Dutch Colonial stone houses of the Hudson Valley and built it of fieldstone taken from stone walls on his property. He also designed numerous features that made it easy for him to use in his wheelchair, making it one of the earliest homes designed to be accessible to a disabled person . Roosevelt found solitude and quiet at Top Cottage, but also liked to entertain visitors there, including King George VI and Queen Elizabeth of England who attended the famous "hotdog" picnic on the porch.

The completion of Top Cottage was one indication that FDR intended to retire in 1940 after two terms. Another was the construction of a library close to Springwood to house his papers and those of other members of his administration. The Franklin Delano Roosevelt Library and Museum was established through legislation authored by Roosevelt and enacted by Congress in 1939. It was the first of the Presidential Libraries, and every president since Roosevelt has created a private foundation, as Roosevelt did, to raise funds to build a library for the papers of his administration—the completed libraries are deeded to the Federal government and then administrated by the National Archives. For its design and construction Roosevelt turned again to the Dutch Colonial style and the native fieldstone that he loved.

After his mother died in 1941, Roosevelt inherited Springwood and made arrangements in his will to make a gift of it to the United States government. Eleanor

ABOVE *The dining room. Gatherings great and small were held here and holidays celebrated, including family Christmases. If the table proved too small, extra tables would be added to the end, a tablecloth stretched over the whole thing, and the folding chairs (seen to the right) employed.*

The silver candelabra (left) were a present to ER from her grandmother. The porcelain wedding party in the center of the table was purchased in Scandinavia by the Roosevelts (on loan from the Presidential Library). On the wall at the right hang Christmas cards from the White House staff to ER after FDR's death until Christmas, 1953. ER thought they were too pretty to put away.

RIGHT *ER's living room in the former Factory Building. ER turned the building into her country home after 1937 and would refer to "The peace of Val-Kill." Her living room decorated in a hodge-podge of comfortable overstuffed chairs, comfortably arranged to make conversation easier—she liked to sit here in the evenings after dinner with her company, famous and infamous.*

Roosevelt and her children were given a life tenancy, but declined it and allowed the property to be transferred to the United States government immediately after the President's death. The home and its contents were left very much as they were at that time.

Eleanor Roosevelt, born in 1884, was the daughter of Elliott Roosevelt and his wife Anna Hall. Her mother died in 1892 and her father in 1894. She spent the rest of her childhood with her maternal grandmother at Oak Lawn near Tivoli, New York, and then attended boarding school in England. She married Franklin Roosevelt in 1905 and was escorted to the altar by her uncle, President Theodore Roosevelt. Eleanor

ABOVE AND TOP RIGHT *The second floor contains three bedrooms and a sleeping porch (top right). They reflect ER's simple taste, furnished with Val-Kill furniture and with the walls of the main bedroom (above) covered with photographs of family and friends. ER's favorite room was the sleeping porch. Her "My Day" columns, syndicated nation-wide, contain frequent references to this room: "I awoke this morning and was happy to see blue sky and the sun just coming over the trees and shining on my sleeping porch." ER often slept there until winter had well set in. Many of the furnishings at Val-Kill were auctioned off after her death in 1962. The property was sold in 1970, to be bought back by the government in 1977 and opened to the public in 1984. Since then there have been many concerted efforts to buy back the furnishings; some have also been donated or given back as well.*

The property was a favorite picnic spot even before it was purchased in 1911 by FDR. After it was bought the stream was dammed to create a pond, called Val-Kill by FDR, for ice skating in the winter and canoeing in the summer. An outdoor fireplace was built in 1933 where ER held countless picnics, and a tennis court added in 1950. The bridge to Val-Kill became known as Mrs. Roosevelts's doorbell because of the clattering sound the planks made.

The grounds were full of flowers: a formal garden was established by Nancy Cook. After she left in 1947 this was not kept up, but the cutting garden was, and ER added a rose garden in 1960. Her routine always included a walk in the garden to cut flowers when she visited Val-Kill for the house and for her apartment in New York City.

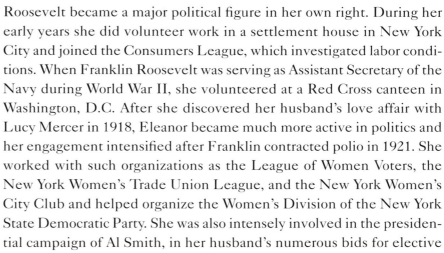

Roosevelt became a major political figure in her own right. During her early years she did volunteer work in a settlement house in New York City and joined the Consumers League, which investigated labor conditions. When Franklin Roosevelt was serving as Assistant Secretary of the Navy during World War II, she volunteered at a Red Cross canteen in Washington, D.C. After she discovered her husband's love affair with Lucy Mercer in 1918, Eleanor became much more active in politics and her engagement intensified after Franklin contracted polio in 1921. She worked with such organizations as the League of Women Voters, the New York Women's Trade Union League, and the New York Women's City Club and helped organize the Women's Division of the New York State Democratic Party. She was also intensely involved in the presidential campaign of Al Smith, in her husband's numerous bids for elective office, and in pushing the progressive agendas of women, blacks, youth, and labor within the Roosevelt administration.

In 1924 Franklin Roosevelt asked Henry Toombs to design a stone cottage in the Dutch Colonial style for his wife and her two associates and friends, Nancy Cook and Marion Dickerman. The three women shared interests in education and in political and social causes, and before construction of the stone cottage was completed, they combined forces to create Val-Kill Industries, an experiment intended to train young men from the neighborhood, particularly farm workers, in the crafts and provide employment. Construction of a furniture factory building began in 1926 and was expanded to include a center for the study of handicrafts; metalwork and a weaving in the years that followed. The Val-Kill Furniture Shop and Forge remained in operation until it went out of business in 1936. Eleanor later converted the factory building into her home.

After Franklin Roosevelt's death, Eleanor Roosevelt purchased Val-Kill and 1,000 acres from his estate and bought out the interest of Cook and Dickerman in the stone cottage. When Springwood was given to the United States government, Val-Kill became the center of life at Hyde Park for her and her family.

Eleanor Roosevelt continued in public life after her husband's death. In 1946, she was appointed by President Truman as a delegate to the United Nations and chaired the UN Commission that drafted the Universal Declaration of Human Rights. She remained an influential voice in the Democratic Party and an active journalist, author, speaker, and advocate for civil rights. As head of the Roosevelt family, she became "Grandmère" to a growing number of grandchildren and great-grandchildren. She died in 1962 and was buried next to her husband in the rose garden at Springwood.

The three Roosevelt houses at Hyde Park, Springwood, Top Cottage and Val-Kill, together with the FDR Library and Museum illustrate the long history of the Roosevelt family in the Hudson River Valley, and the role that Franklin and Eleanor Roosevelt played on the national and international stage. They are administered by the National Park Service as part of the Roosevelt National Historic Site, and are open to the public.

OPPOSITE In the center of the picture one can see the Rose Garden, burial place by the choice of FDR, for ER and himself. Visitors are often hushed and humbled as they walk through his mother's Rose Garden. Behind the Vermont marble tombstone is a sun dial: at the base rests "Fala," a black Scottie dog, probably the most famous Presidential dog ever, and "Chief," a dog belonging to the Roosevelt's oldest child and only daughter Anna.

Locust Grove

Samuel Finley Breese Morse was born in Charleston in 1791. He attended Yale College and studied art at The Royal Academy in London, which at that time was under the aegis of the American-born Benjamin West, president of the Royal Academy for thirty years. In London West acted as mentor to many young American artists, including John Singleton Copley, Charles Willson Peale, Gilbert Stuart, and Washington Allston. Morse moved to New York in 1823, where he supported himself through portraiture and achieved distinction as a painter of large genre scenes, the best known being the architectural rendering of the old House of Representatives. Morse helped in founding the National Academy of Design in 1826 and served as its first president. While painting brought Morse a measure of fame, it was his invention of the telegraph that brought him fortune. He developed the Morse code, obtained funds from Congress to build an experimental telegraph line from Washington to Baltimore, and on this line, in 1844, demonstrated the utility of the new invention. Morse gave up painting to pursue this new enterprise and with the financial security it brought was able to buy Locust Grove.

The verandah was a pleasant spot for outdoor relaxation and views of the garden framed by pilasters trimmed with lattice.

RIGHT Locust Grove's Tuscan tower was a landmark, easily seen from the steamboats on the Hudson River.

This property was purchased in 1751 by Henry Livingston, a surveyor and clerk of Dutchess County, who was also a grandson of Robert Livingston, first Lord of Livingston Manor. He sold it to his son, Henry Livingston, Jr., who built a house, a sawmill and wharf, and farmed the land. It was Livingston who named this place Locust Grove after the picturesque black locust trees that grew there in abundance. In 1830 John and Isabella Montgomery, a rich New York couple, bought Locust Grove and replaced Livingston's farmhouse with a new Federal-style house, carefully sited

LEFT *The dining room is the centerpiece of the north wing added to Locust Grove in 1901 by the Youngs. It replaced a much smaller dining room (today the music room) used by the Morses that was too small for the grand parties envisioned by the Youngs. The long mahogany table (American, c. 1840) extends to seat up to twelve guests and is surrounded by Federal lyre-back chairs (American, c. 1815). Three New York sideboards, two with inlaid satinwood stringing and bellflowers, hold Tiffany silver and Meissen porcelain used by the family. Portraits of William and Martha Young by Josef Koppay (c. 1911) flank the fireplace, while a portrait of William Young's grandfather, Henry Young, by Samuel L. Waldo (c.1860) occupies the place of honor over the mantel.*

ABOVE *The drawing room is the most formal reception room at Locust Grove. Occupying the entire first floor of the great Tuscan tower added by Morse and Davis in 1851, this room is placed on axis with the front door and entrance hall. Through the tall casement windows the great sweep of the West lawn leads the eye toward the Hudson River and distant hills, a dramatic vista created by Samuel Morse. The drawing room is furnished with a group of white painted and gilt decorated furniture (American, c.1815) and a large gilt pier mirror (American, c. 1850) that the Youngs acquired from the Morse family when they bought the house. A part of Martha Young's extensive collection of transfer-decorated cups and Staffordshire plates is displayed in the massive Chippendale secretary (American, c. 1750), while a 19th-century copy of Titian's "Flora" hangs over the mantel.*

on the edge of a steep bluff to take advantage of the views of the Hudson to the north and south. It was during the Montgomery's tenure that Locust Grove changed from a working farm to a genteel country estate.

Samuel Morse bought Locust Grove in 1847, and a year later married his cousin, Sarah Elizabeth Griswold, who happened to be a great-granddaughter of Henry Livingston, Jr. Morse then prepared numerous sketches of the existing house to develop his ideas for the extensive alterations that he had in mind. To help him with this enterprise, he engaged his friend, the architect Alexander J. Davis. Together they worked to prepare an architectural design: their collaboration might be compared in some ways to that of the architect Calvert Vaux and the painter Frederic Church at Olana some twenty years later.

Alexander J. Davis was born in New York but spent much of his childhood in upstate New York and New Jersey. As a young man, he worked as a typesetter for his brother in Alexandria, Virginia. He returned to New York (in the same year that Samuel Morse moved there) to study drawing and painting, and became known for

ABOVE *Library. Added in 1851, this half-octagonal room was designed by Morse as his study. From a large oak desk in the center of the room, Morse could enjoy the lovely view across the wide veranda to the flower beds that surround the house. After the Youngs moved to Locust Grove, they installed the glass-fronted Gothic Revival bookcases and filled them with reference books, histories, and novels. Furnishings include the papier-mâché work table, writing desk, and table, all c. 1850.*

LEFT *Conveniently located across the entrance hall from the parlors, this room was used as the dining room until 1901 when the Youngs added a larger and more modern room in the new north wing. Annette and Innis Young studied music on the piano, recorders, and mandolins displayed in this room and also staged recitals here for their friends and parents. The furnishings in this room include a large group of Elizabethan Revival library furniture (New York, c. 1850) made for Henry Winthrop Sargent's estate, Wodenethe, in Beacon. Two large gilt bull's-eye mirrors (American, c. 1830), originally with convex mirror plates, flank a three-quarter length portrait of Hasbrouck Innis (Mrs. Young's brother) by Josef Koppay (c. 1911).*

RIGHT *The billiards room, with its domed ceiling and Palladian window, is one of the most imposing architectural spaces at Locust Grove. While Morse designed the room as an integral part of his 1851 renovations, no record survives for its use before the Morse family sold the estate in 1900. The Youngs moved in a billiards table (manufactured by the Brunswick-Balke-Collender Company in the 1890s). Mr. Young was an avid billiards player, and his trophies from tournaments at the Union League Club in New York City line the tops of the highboys (American, c.1740-1760) flanking the east window. Other significant pieces of furniture include a large mahogany wardrobe (English, c. 1720) now used as a bookcase and the group of eight framed lithographs of Plains Indians by George Catlin.*

his architectural renderings before he determined, some time around 1829, to practice architecture.

Davis knew Morse when he was a student at the National Academy of Design and from the numerous evenings when artists were invited to socialize at Morse's home and studio on

Canal Street. They became friends, as evidenced by Morse's small oil panel, depicting a romantic house sitting in a picturesque landscape, which Davis used as the title vignette for his book *Rural Residences*.

Furnished much as it appeared in 1908, Annette Young's bedroom was used by her from 1895 until she moved to the master bedroom after her mother's death in 1946. The wonderful views of the Hudson River and the glimpses of wildlife from the window must have made this room a favorite for Annette, a nature and animal enthusiast. Personal photographs and mementos fill the room, and the furnishings include a large secretary (American, c. 1810) for Annette's books and correspondence and a chest of drawers (American, c. 1825).

RIGHT Guest bedroom suite. Comprising two bedrooms on the east side of the house with connecting closets and a dressing room, the guest suite was completed during the Young family's renovations in 1900. With the interior doors closed, these rooms could be used separately or thrown together as required. Hasbrouck Innis, Mrs. Young's brother, used these rooms frequently; the large wardrobes and chests of drawers were also used by the Youngs to store out-of-season clothing and linens and the rooms served as a playroom for the children.

Davis and other architects in the mid-19th century made a cottage industry altering Georgian and Federal-style houses to bring them into conformity with current fashion. Examples of Hudson River Valley houses changed in this way include Davis's work at Montgomery Place and Edgewater, Washington Irving's transformation of Sunnyside, and the alterations made by others at Clermont and Rokeby.

At Locust Grove, Davis and Morse started with the rectangular shape of the original house, added bays to the north and south, and a porte-cochere to the east. On the west front they built a four-story Tuscan tower facing the river, which was so prominent that it became a landmark for the tourists traveling by steamboat on the river.

Morse spent the next two decades refining the landscape at Locust Grove planting trees, moving walls, and laying out flower gardens. He continued to pursue his interests in the telegraph, and litigated over his patent rights, which were finally confirmed by a Supreme Court decision in 1854. During the last years of his life he worked with Peter Cooper and Cyrus W. Field to lay the first transatlantic telegraph cable. Morse died in 1872, and his wife in 1901, and in that year their heirs sold Locust Grove to William and Martha Young, a New York couple with extensive social ties in Poughkeepsie.

By 1900, the Youngs had already rented Locust Grove for five summers and immediately began to update the house to make it a comfortable, full-time residence. They demolished Morse's half-octagonal north wing, added a new dining room and bedrooms, and installed steam heat, electric lights, and new plumbing fixtures. William and Martha Young had an avid interest in the decorative arts, and filled Locust Grove with their collection of furniture, paintings, and porcelain. Their daughter, Annette Innis Young, saw to Locust Grove's designation as a National Historic Landmark in 1963 and on her death, in 1975, a private foundation was established to preserve the house, grounds, and collection, in accordance with her wishes, for the "enjoyment, visitation, and enlightenment of the public."

ABOVE Aerial view showing the West lawn. The landscape design of the estate is essentially that which Samuel Morse perceived.

BELOW As seen from the West porch, with the clearing of the trees that had grown together to obscure the view, the Hudson River is now visible again.

Madam Brett Homestead

A devout member of the Dutch Reformed Church, Catheryna Brett is said to have prayed daily. It is not surprising that she donated the land on which the Fishkill Reformed Church would be built, and in the cemetery of which she would be buried. On display at the Homestead is Catheryna's own sermon book, printed in 1747 in Boston. The inscription on its frontispiece reads, "Catheryna Brett, Her Book. When you have Read it unto the End pray Send it home. I Did it Lend."

Nodding flowers, period herbs, and gravel paths grace the restored Dutch garden that adjoins the circa 1709 Madam Brett Homestead. Located in the heart of the City of Beacon, the property now comprises about six acres of land—a small fraction of the Bretts' patent share of nearly 28,000 acres. First constructed to take advantage of the natural light through a southern exposure, the home's front and back entrances were reversed when the village grew up to the property's back door. Today the original front entrance of the home is the rear entry, facing the garden.

The development of land in Dutchess County occurred along lines that were somewhat different from Westchester, Putnam, Columbia, and Albany counties. There the land was generally formed into large manors and granted with feudal privileges to owners who rented their land under long-term leases. In Dutchess County, most of the land was first purchased under ten Crown patents, granted between 1685 and 1706 to well-connected speculators, most of whom subdivided their land and sold it to independent freeholders. Dutchmen, Germans, Huguenots, and Walloons settled the area nearest to the river. Settlers from New England moved into the eastern half. It was this pattern that gave Dutchess County its unique character.

Catheryna Rombout Brett was the daughter of a Walloon father and Dutch mother and was married to a British naval lieutenant. It was said that she spoke a mixture of Dutch and English. Her father, Francis Rombout, was once the mayor of New York. In 1683, he and his partners negotiated to purchase from the Wappingers Indians all the land lying between the Fish Kill and the Wappingers Kill, east from the Hudson, "into the woods, fouer houers goeing," land which amounted to 85,000 acres. Of this, Catheryna and Roger Brett inherited 28,000 acres, and in 1708 they built a gristmill at the mouth of the Fishkill Creek.

The Bretts set aside acreage for a homestead, in what is now the city of Beacon, and hired a carpenter to build a house. They made plans to develop their land, but in 1718 Roger Brett was knocked overboard by the boom of a sloop as it entered the Fishkill Creek and drowned. His body was carried to land by his manservant and his remains buried in the small family burial ground. Catheryna Brett was left with three young children and serious financial obligations, some of them to the Secretary of the Province of New York, George Clarke. He was a chivalrous man who helped Catheryna Brett set her finances in order. She sold large tracts to those willing to settle her land, and families such as the Brinckerhoffs, the Van Wycks, and the Storms came from Long Island to settle in the shadows of the Hudson Highlands and to farm the rich soil of southern Dutchess County.

Catheryna Brett was the only European woman living amidst 28,000 acres of wilderness. With the help of a few slaves, she remained on her land and expanded the

LEFT AND ABOVE The summer kitchen is located in the oldest portion of the Homestead and filled with the cooking implements of yesterday, from a beehive oven and massive hearth to a cooking crane and pie safe. Also on display in the kitchen is a reproduction riding coat and hat, like those that Madam Brett herself might have worn. She was an avid horsewoman who is said to have ridden over her property on horseback daily. Though Catheryna was a successful businesswoman, the owner of several slaves, and the mother of three surviving sons, she would have also been charged with running a large household — directing menus and food preparation on the estate, as well as dispensing medical cures through the use of herbs from her adjoining garden.

mill at the mouth of the creek. It was successful, and farmers brought their grain from as far away as Goshen. The saying went, "all roads lead to Madam Brett's mill." Her properties were cleared and farmed, and she founded and became the largest shareholder of the Frankfort Storehouse, a cooperative of farmers, which sent its crops to Manhattan for sale. She lived and worked alongside the local Wappingers Indians, whom she allowed to remain on her lands, and counted Chief Sachem Daniel Ninham as a friend.

Catheryna Brett was an astute businesswoman, and to limit competition to her mill, put restrictions in her land transactions which prohibited buyers from building their own mills. She reserved future mineral rights for herself and took adversaries to court over disputed boundaries and perceived encroachments. She had little formal education, willfully chose to remain a widow, and made her way against all odds.

She died in 1764, and was buried in the churchyard of the Dutch Reformed Church in Fishkill. Her son Francis Brett and his wife, Catharine Van Wyck, raised eight children in the house. Their daughter Hannah married Henry Schenck and they lived in the house with their own nine children. During the American Revolution, Henry Schenck was a major in Swartout's regiment and quartermaster for the local troops. Rations of supplies were stored in the Homestead's cellar and soldiers slept in rows on the floors. During the Revolution, Major and Hannah Schenck entertained General Washington, the Marquis de Lafayette, and Baron Von Steuben. It is said they all danced the minuet in the drawing room with Major Schenck's daughters.

Seven generations of Catheryna Brett's descendants lived in the house. But by 1954, no family member was willing or able to take on the upkeep of the house and it was sold to The Great Atlantic and Pacific Tea Company, Inc. to be demolished and

A large collection of Chinese trade porcelain and fine silverware is displayed in the dining room of the Homestead. The china in the small, wall-mounted cabinet is believed to be that of Madam Brett and bears her armorial crest. The furnishings on display at the Homestead, which was inhabited by seven successive generations of the Brett family, illustrate the evolution of style. Like the adjacent drawing room, the dining room has a decidedly Federal-style influence. Though many of the pieces on display are original to the Homestead, many others were donated by members of the local community and the Melzingah Chapter of the Daughters of the American Revolution, who saved the house from demolition in 1954.

In 1790, Isaac De Peyster Teller married Alice Schenck and they and their six children became the fourth generation to reside in the Homestead. The Tellers exerted a strong influence on its character, and introduced Federal-style moldings and mantelpiece to the main drawing room. In time, Isaac became a member of Congress, a country squire and a generous benefactor to the local community. Until the 1950s, the house would be called Teller's Villa, and the front-door knocker still bears the Teller name.

replaced by a supermarket. The local community rallied behind the Melzingah Chapter of the Daughters of the American Revolution to save the house and property. Through the proceeds of bake sales, card parties, and outright donations, the Daughters raised the funds needed to rescue the house in which they had received their chapter charter in 1896. In honor of Catheryna Brett's courageous life, the Chapter christened its new home The Madam Brett Homestead.

   This house is the oldest building standing in Dutchess County and an outstanding example of early Dutch architecture. It is one-and-a-half stories high, with shed dormers on a gently peaked roof. Many of the old

The Homestead's Slocum bedroom is furnished with tiger maple furniture, all fine pieces which might have decorated the private chambers of a landed Hudson River family at the time of the American Revolution. The dormer that now admits afternoon sunshine into this upstairs room was not original and was probably added around the turn of the 20th century. Madam Brett's handmade doll dates to approximately 1685 and is one of several personal effects, including her shoes and pewter miniature tea set, also on display.

hand-scalloped wood shake shingles remain, as do the massive interior timbers. The original floorboards and hand-wrought hardware are among the many notable features of this house, which was considered a mansion when compared to the more modest homes built nearby. In the early 19th century, Federal-style moldings and mantels were installed, leaded glass placed over the entrance doors, and the main entrance changed from the south side to the north. Over the years there have been many other alterations as each generation left its mark on the house.

Today, the Madam Brett Homestead continues a long tradition of hospitality, welcoming 1,000 visitors a year, many of them schoolchildren who have their first encounter with local history, as well as the story of the remarkable Catheryna Rombout Brett.

A splendid example of the Federal style of architecture, Boscobel combines supreme elegance with spare simplicity. Though its architect was unknown, he was clearly familiar with and influenced by current English trends, notably by the late 18th-century neoclassicist Robert Adam and by Samuel and James Wyatt, originators of the unique triple "Wyatt window," four of which are featured in Boscobel's façade. Set originally near Montrose on a site overlooking the Hudson, Boscobel was so named by its builder, States Morris Dyckman, a lifelong Anglophile, for the Forest of Boscobel in which the future King Charles II hid from his enemies during the English civil wars. Slated for destruction in the mid 1950s, the home was moved to Garrison, a glorious site on the Hudson worthy of the house itself. The superb siting of the house can be understood looking from theurns which sit at the edge of the front lawn (opposite bottom). The view is straight down the Hudson River.

Boscobel

The house is distinguished by its delicate exterior neoclassical detailing, as well as for a unique architectural feature on the front façade—the carved wooden swags of drapery with bowknots and tassels installed between the columns supporting the pediment above the second floor balcony. One-third of the front façade of Boscobel is glass: three-part windows are used on the first and second stories with slightly larger individual window-panes made possible due to then technological advances in glassmaking allowing for larger and stronger panes of glass to me made which could be supported by thinner glazing bars. This helps to convey a feeling of lightness and airiness which makes the house seem more graceful and sophisticated than many of its contemporaries.

oscobel is the most elegant neoclassical house from the Federal period to be built along the Hudson River. It is interesting both for the history of its construction and also for the circumstances of its rescue, relocation and restoration. States Morris Dyckman began the construction of the house in the early 19th century, on his farm overlooking the Haverstraw Bay, south of Montrose. Beginning in 1956, it was rebuilt on its present site in Garrison, a site with equally splendid views, about fifteen miles north of the original, and is now considered one of the nation's leading historic house museums, with an important collection of decorative arts from the Federal period.

States Morris Dyckman was a farm boy, born in the Bronx in 1755, descended from one of New York's early Dutch families. Like many before and after him , he dreamed of the life of a country gentleman. He was a staunch Loyalist during the American Revolution, and a clerk for the

States Dyckman died long before the completion of Boscobel, but his widow, Elizabeth, faithfully forged ahead with the plans for their dream house. Above is her bedroom and over the mantel hangs a portrait of Peter, their only surviving child (c. 1805). The impressive high-post mahogany bedstead is one of a very few known to be from the workshop of Duncan Phyfe, the leading New York designer and cabinetmaker of the early 19th century. The bed hangings are of green silk and the curtains of white cotton, a fabric much favored in the Federal period.

British army's Quartermaster Department in New York, which was responsible for providing provisions and supplies to the British army. Dyckman was in charge of the accounts, and in 1779, accompanied the quartermasters to London for a government audit. He stayed there for the duration of the investigation until 1789, when the charges were dismissed, and was well rewarded for his services. Dyckman then returned to New York, endowed with sufficient funds to set himself up in Montrose, to begin a new life as a gentleman farmer.

In 1794, Dyckman married Elizabeth Corne, the granddaughter of a rich Loyalist neighbor, Peter Corne. There was a twenty-one-year age difference (he was thirty-nine and she eighteen), but their correspondence indicated a love match. Their happiness must have been strained, however, by Dyckman's chronic financial difficulties. He lived beyond his means and was excessively generous to family members who suffered losses during the Revolution. At one point, he sold his collection of leather-bound books to Chancellor Livingston to raise funds. In 1795, payments from the annuity stopped. Dyckman sailed to London in 1799 to reassert his claim, and while there, was called upon to assist General John Dalrymple, the last of the quartermasters under investigation. All of this kept him away until 1803, but during this visit, he managed to have payments from his annuity resumed and received large settlements from General Dalrymple and other quartermasters he had helped.

The upstairs sitting room contains several of Boscobel's finest pieces of furniture. Both the drum-shaped writing table and the mahogany breakfront are attributed to Duncan Phyfe and his workshop (1810-20). States and his wife were forced to live apart for several years while he worked in England, but many of the letters that Elizabeth wrote to him during their separation—perhaps on a table similar to this one—have been preserved. The breakfront, commissioned by the New York lawyer Thomas Witter Chrystie, bears the Chrystie crest and is thought to be the first piece of furniture made in this country decorated with a family crest. Above the table is the fanciful Mercury chandelier (c. 1807), probably the design of the neoclassicist William Holland.

Dyckman returned to New York financially secure but ill from persistent attacks of gout and the lingering effects of a carriage accident. Regardless, he was determined to build the house he had dreamed of, to symbolize his status, display his taste, and create a permanent seat that would be left to future generations. Construction began in the summer of 1804, but only the foundation was complete when in 1806, Dyckman died at the age of fifty-one. His widow, Elizabeth Dyckman, finished the house, and moved there in 1808 with her only surviving child. In years to come the house was left to this child, Peter Corne Dyckman, and then by him to his daughter, Eliza Letitia Dyckman and her husband, John Peach Cruger.

The designer of Boscobel is not known, but the design of the south elevation is distinctive. The triple windows, set into niches, were uncommon in America at this time, suggesting an English influence. There they were known as "Wyatt windows," after

ABOVE *The portrait of Dr. James Henderson and his daughters, hanging in the stair hall, is one of the oldest paintings in the collection, c. 1726. Henderson, a New York physician and merchant, was also the great-grandfather of Elizabeth Dyckman. The painting is attributed to John Watson, a Scotsman who emigrated to New Jersey. On the second-floor landing stands the finest wardrobe in the Boscobel collection. This piece of furniture, attributed to the Duncan Phyfe workshop, along with the breakfront in the upstairs sitting room (page 137), were the two most expensive pieces of furniture listed in the 1810 New York Price Book.*

Above the wardrobe is "Narcissus," one of the most highly praised mythological paintings of Benjamin West, a Pennsylvania-born artist who was also court painter to King George III.

ABOVE *The silver-plated hot water urn in the center of the front drawing room is among the first of Dyckman's English purchases to be shipped home (in 1788). With its elegant, understated form, it is an early example of the pure classical style, then the height of fashion in England, but perhaps among the first of its kind to reach these shores. It is monogrammed with Dyckman's initials and hints at the elegant life the bachelor was imagining for himself back on his New York farm. The curule chairs (Duncan Phyfe, 1810-20) are embellished with scroll backs and seaweed carvings.*

the English architect Samuel Wyatt and his son James, who used them in their designs as a kind of trademark at the end of the 18th century. These windows intrude into the bracketed cornice, which achieves its full height only above the elegant attenuated pilasters. The pediment has a low pitch, with a fanlight topped by swags, the kind that was sometimes used in Venetian windows in New England and also found in the pediment of the Congregational Church at Old Lyme, Connecticut. The columns that support this pediment are connected by carved wood drapery, with knots and tassels. Many of these same elements can be seen on other houses of the period, but here they are combined with great style and elegance and leave the impression of a supremely self-confident designer.

In the 1950s the federal government bought the site and built a hospital. The house was declared "excess" by the federal government and sold at auction to a demolition contractor for $35, who in turn sold the south façade and many other architectural details to be used in a house on Long Island. In a dramatic, last-ditch effort led by Benjamin West Frazier, funds were raised to acquire the remaining portions of the

ABOVE *In 1803 Dyckman finally settled his accounts in England, assuring himself and his family a handsome income. He celebrated by purchasing twenty caseloads of furnishings for the home he now planned to build along the Hudson. In one of these cases was the stunning pair of candelabra that today stand on the Boscobel dining room table. These are the finest of the remaining Dyckman possessions. Around the table are painted "bamboo" chairs like those his wife Elizabeth bought for the dining room. The table is set with plates and compotiers that are part of the "rich dessert service" English, Coalport porcelain, "painted in landscapes to order" purchased by States Dyckman from Sharpus and Co., London, September 24, 1803.*

structure, dismantle and store them. Many of the pieces sent to Long Island were retrieved, including the distinctive wood drapery of the south façade. In 1956, a donation from Lila Acheson Wallace allowed the newly incorporated Boscobel Restoration, Inc. to buy a sixteen-acre site in Garrison, on which the house was rebuilt.

Mrs. Wallace, who had co-founded The Reader's Digest Association, Inc. with her husband DeWitt Wallace, became Boscobel's most prominent and generous patron. In addition to financial backing, she served on the Board of Directors and took a strong personal interest in the restoration of the house and the design of the landscape. The rooms were decorated and furnished with English antiques, and a plan prepared for the grounds, with elegant formal gardens, designed by Richard K. Webel. On May 21, 1961, the reconstructed house was formally opened to the public.

By the mid-1970s, new information came to light about States Dyckman's original furnishings that led to the decision to totally redesign the interiors to make them more historically accurate. Information found in the Dyckman family papers, a newly discovered household inventory of 1806, and examples of surviving furniture owned by the Dyckman family revealed that Boscobel was originally furnished with pieces

The tranquil formal gardens of Boscobel mirror the elegant lines of the Federal house. This serene setting belies the turmoil of more than fifty years ago when the home was narrowly rescued from the wrecking ball and carted off piece by piece to its new location. Boscobel stands today—on a stunning piece of land overlooking the Hudson to both the south and west—a testament to the valiant efforts of its many friends and supporters.

made in New York in the early 19th century. Berry B. Tracy, then Curator-in-Charge of the American Wing at the Metropolitan Museum of Art, was hired as a consultant to research the new interiors and oversee the installation. Tracy replaced the English pieces with an outstanding collection of Federal period furniture, made mostly by New York cabinet-makers, including Duncan Phyfe. Many of States Dyckman's original purchases of English china, silver, glass and part of his library have survived and are on exhibit in the house. Reproduction carpeting, paint colors, wallpaper, fabrics and window treatments, based upon documented period examples, were installed. This reinterpretation restored the house to the way it might have looked when

Elizabeth Dyckman lived there from 1808 until her death in 1823. The house reopened to the public in June of 1977, after six months of intense restoration work.

Van Cortlandt Manor

In 1609 Henry Hudson, an English captain sailing on behalf of the Dutch East India Company, undertook the first exploration of the Hudson River. He sailed all the way to Albany in a failed search for a northerly passage to Asia, but reported to his financial backers his perception of the potential for fur trading. The East India Company was not impressed by these reports and sent him on another quest, ending in his death at Hudson Bay. However, Hudson's reports were of interest to others in Amsterdam who dispatched trading ships, beginning in 1610.

In 1621 the Dutch West India Company was chartered and took possession of the colony, naming it New Netherland, and in March of 1623 they furnished a ship to carry to this new land a party of about thirty families, mostly French-speaking Walloons in search of religious freedom. In 1626 the Company purchased the island of Manhattan from the Indians and built Fort Amsterdam as an inducement to future colonists.

The settlers came, seeking religious freedom and prosperity, and the colony slowly grew. Among the immigrants was Oloff Stevense, from Holland, a soldier in the employ of The Dutch West India Company, who arrived in 1638. Stevense married Annetje Loockermans in 1642 and elevated his station by becoming a brewer and involving himself in the politics of the colony. He achieved a success sufficient to embolden him to add to his surname the aristocratic suffix Van Cortlandt.

A son, Stephanus Van Cortlandt was born in 1643. He continued in the tradition of his father, mixing business and politics, and adapting easily, in 1664, when the Duke of York seized New Netherland for the English. Stephanus was chosen as the first

The dining room (right) and parlor (above) contain an important collection of Queen Anne, Chippendale, and Federal-style furniture. The Chinese export porcelain and the Chelsea and Chelsea-Derby figurines were also Van Cortlandt family possessions.

native-born mayor of New York in 1677 and again from 1686 to 1688. He served as commander of the Kings County Militia, as judge in the Colonial and Admiralty courts, and as Senior Warden at Trinity Parish. It was this combination of commercial endeavor, political connection, and religious affiliation that enabled the Van Cortlandts to achieve great status. By 1687 Stephanus had acquired 85,000 acres of land in upper Westchester County, purchased from European landowners and from the Kitchtawanc Indians. In 1697 he received a Royal Charter confirming title to this property, incorporating it as the Manor of Cortlandt, with a provision allowing for its inheritance under the law of primogeniture.

As proprietor of this estate, he was encouraged to develop it and to lease portions of it to settlers who would cultivate the land and increase its value. But the system was less than successful, for the obvious reason that the leaseholder could never obtain permanent title to the land he had improved, a cause for the young, ambitious, and energetic to look to Rockland, Orange, or Dutchess County, or wherever a freehold title might be obtained. It is a measure of the failure of the manorial system that in 1748, when Stephanus' son Philip Van Cortlandt died, his portion of the Van Cortlandt Manor contained only six tenant families.

Tradition holds that in 1687 when Stephanus Van Cortlandt completed his land

The Manor's milk room (above) and kitchen (right) are on the ground level. The milk room provides natural cool storage space for meat, vegetables, cheese, and dairy products. The kitchen contains a huge fireplace with hearth extending well into the room, and a beehive oven in the back. This kitchen is one of the largest and best equipped colonial period kitchens in America.

acquisitions, there stood along the Hudson River on the north side of the Croton a rude stone building that had been used as a fort and trading post, with thick walls of red sandstone. According to tradition, the Van Cortlandts converted this rudimentary building into a dwelling house, but from 1687 until 1749, the family remained in New York City and used the Westchester house as an outpost to conduct the business of the Manor.

In 1700 Stephanus Van Cortlandt died and his heirs held the Manor in common title. In 1734 when the estate was divided among his ten children, his son Philip Van Cortlandt inherited the portion immediately north of the Croton River, the portion on which the stone house stood. Philip Van Cortlandt had business affairs in New York and little use for the Westchester property. When he died in 1748, his son Pierre Van Cortlandt inherited what had become an undeveloped and unprofitable tract of land while Pierre's older brother received more profitable property in Manhattan. Heavily in debt and with no other opportunities, the Manor was Pierre's only asset.

That year he married Joanna Livingston, and in 1749 they left New York and made the Croton house their permanent residence, the home where they raised their eight children. Together they developed the Manor and attracted tenants by giving them

The Ferry House (right) was a tenant farmhouse, inn and tavern, serving visitors traveling on the Albany Post Road which passed by this building. Inside is a collection of 18th century New York furniture, English ceramics, and other objects. An outstanding collection of pewter, mostly American, fills the tap room (above).

leases on generous terms. They maintained a ferry across the Croton and operated a sawmill and a gristmill. Pierre worked as a transportation agent, land developer, rent collector, landlord, commercial farmer, and tavern owner. As a result of these efforts the Van Cortlandts prospered, and in 1758 added 3,138 acres to the original 1,225.

The Revolutionary War and the British occupation of New York interrupted their idyllic life. Westchester County became a "neutral ground" between the British troops in New York and the American forces in the upstate region. Pierre Van Cortlandt was active in politics, serving in the second, third, and fourth Provincial Congresses and having to choose sides, determined to support the Colonies in their rebellion. He and his family fled upstate to Rhinebeck. Naturally, the manor house was the subject of attacks and by the time the family returned at war's end only the shell of the house remained.

Rebuilding began, and in 1814 Pierre

There are two bedchambers on the second level of the manor, separated by the center hall. The Northwest room (above) came to be known as the Prophet's Chamber, as it was offered to itinerant Methodist ministers regularly calling on the Van Cortlandts, who were converts to Methodism. Almost all the furnishing of the Northeast room (opposite) including the cast-iron stove, are original. The fabrics in both rooms were reproduced from scraps of the originals found during the restoration.

Van Cortlandt died and was succeeded by his son, General Philip Van Cortlandt, a veteran of the Continental Army and a member of Congress for sixteen years. He served as a Commissioner of Forfeiture and as such, was responsible for the confiscation of landholdings of those families in New York City who, unlike the Van Cortlandts, chose the English side in the Revolutionary War. He died in 1831, and the house passed to his brother, Pierre Van Cortlandt, Jr., and then to his son, Pierre Van Cortlandt III. The Van Cortlandts made numerous additions throughout the 19th century, and lived there, using it as their family home, until 1945, a remarkable example of continuous family ownership.

The house and five surrounding acres were purchased in 1953 by John D. Rockefeller, Jr. who commissioned the staff of Colonial Williamsburg to rescue the property and restore it to the period between the Revolutionary War and the War of 1812. In 1959 title was transferred to Sleepy Hollow Restorations, now known as Historic Hudson Valley, which operates Van Cortlandt Manor as a house museum and educational facility. With later land purchases, the protected area is now over 100 acres.

Philipsburg Manor
and the Upper Mills

Fredryck Flypsen came to New Amsterdam from the Netherlands around 1653 to make his fortune, and worked as a master builder for the Dutch West India Company. In 1657, his status advanced from craftsman to merchant when he obtained the Small Burgher Right, after which he began to trade and invest in real estate. In 1662, he married Margaret Hardenbroeck De Vries, a widow with a much greater fortune than his own and an independent woman who traded internationally on her own account. Two years later, when the English administration replaced the Dutch, Flypsen anglicized his name as Philipse and swore allegiance to the English Crown in order to carry on with their business.

Frederick and Margaret Philipse were partners in trade as well as in marriage, engaging in shipping ventures to Europe and the West Indies, and at times conspiring with the pirates based in Madagascar who managed the slave trade. From the profits of their ventures, they bought land, a great deal of it. There were thousands of acres in Albany, Orange and Dutchess counties and thousands more in New Jersey. To this Frederick Philipse added land above Manhattan, land he acquired from Native American and European owners. This land covered a third of what is now Westchester County, and stretched for twenty-two miles along the Hudson River, north from Spuyten Duyvil to the Croton River, east to the Bronx River, 52,000 acres all together. In 1693, King William and Queen Mary granted Philipse a royal charter creating Philipsburg Manor. This charter legitimized Philipse's title to his Westchester estate and capped his career as an entrepreneur, merchant, landowner, ship-owner and slave trader, a career that made him one of the richest men in the colony.

His mill site on the Pocantico River came to be called the Upper Mills to distinguish it from parts of the estate farther down the Hudson, including the Lower Mills in Yonkers, which were established around the same time. The center of the Philipse family enterprise was their house and warehouse in lower Manhattan, now long gone, and the Upper Mills was their northernmost trading and commercial center. Much of the land on Philipsburg Manor was divided into parcels of 150 to 200 acres and rented under long-term leases to tenant farmers, a multi-cultural collection of Swiss, French Huguenots, Dutch Walloons, and Englishmen. Tenants paid their rent in produce or wheat, and brought grain to the Upper Mills to be ground into flour, which was then shipped to other colonies to Europe, and to the Caribbean.

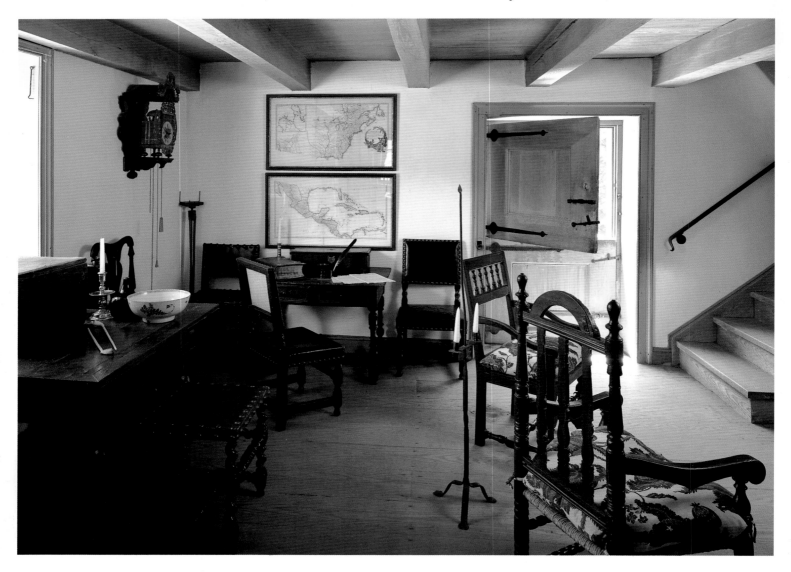

Philipsburg Manor was in reality a commercial outpost for the Philipse family's international trading interests headquartered in New York City. The room above is interpreted as an office, complete with maps, writing instruments, and books. The William and Mary period furniture is English and American. The parlor, right, adjacent to the office, contains an extraordinary painted cupboard made in the Netherlands in the 18th century and painted with scenes from the Apocryhpha. The important collection of Chinese export porcelain, portions of which are visible in the photograph, contains in other rooms the earliest pieces ever found in the colony of New York. The furnishings in these two rooms, like the others in the eight room structure, were collected largely in the 1960s and reflect the inventory of the house made in 1750.

In the middle of the 18th century, slavery was institutionalized throughout much of the British Empire. Slavery was legal in every American colony, and the story of slavery in the north has yet to be fully told. The Philipse's made use of slave labor on their ships and in their New York warehouse. African slaves operated the Upper Mills; perhaps some of whom had been transported on the Philipse's ships. On and off for some twenty years, Frederick Philipse and his son, Adolph Philipse, pursued the transatlantic slave trade and imported hundreds of men and women from different parts of West Africa and Madagascar to the New World. Some were brought to New York, but most were sent to the sugar islands of Barbados, Curacao and Jamaica. The Philipse family's involvement in the slave trade was not entirely successful, due to their circumvention of British maritime law. One of their ship captains narrowly escaped hanging, a ship and two valuable cargoes were confiscated, and Frederick Philipse and his son were barred from holding public office for years.

When Frederick Philipse died in 1702, his son, Adolph Philipse, inherited the northern half of the manor, including the Upper Mills, which he operated until his death in 1750. Adolph Philipse's nephew, Frederick Philipse II, inherited the property and left it in turn to his son, Frederick Philipse III, a loyalist who fled to England after the American Revolution. His estate, including Philipsburg Manor, was confiscated, broken up into nearly 300 parcels, and sold by the Commissioners of Forfeiture to repay New York's war debt. The Van Cortlandt family sided with the colonies, and

ABOVE AND RIGHT
The working, water-powered gristmill was reconstructed on the site of the original Philipse mill, located by archeologists. The impounded Pocantico River provides the power that turns the wheel.

OPPOSITE This barn is an 18th-century structure brought to the site from upstate New York. It is still in daily use as housing for animals and as interpretive space for educational programs. Two oxen pull the wagon (shown) needed for farm operations.

ABOVE. *This room, interpreted as Adolph Philipse's bedchamber, contains colonial American furnishings, including Boston leather chairs, made in Boston about 1710 for export to other colonies, and an easy chair made circa 1710-20.*

OPPOSITE *This view of Philipsburg Manor shows the layout of the commercial complex, with the whitewashed fieldstone Manor House in the center. Adjacent to the Manor is a garden interpreted as a slaves' garden, planted with vegetables, tobacco, medicinal herbs, and other useful plants. On the left is the water-powered mill. The dam which impounds the Pocantico River gives the appearance of being a wooden dam, with a pedestrian walkway connecting the historic area with the modern visitor center. In the middle ground are the barn, reconstructed tenant farmhouse, and fields. The photograph clearly shows how close Philipsburg Manor is to the Hudson River. In the 18th century, the Pocantico River emptied into a harbor, now filled, which made Philipsburg Manor easily accessible to ships. Vessels tied up at the dock next to the mill. Here, they would unload goods brought from elsewhere, and take on agricultural products and flour ground at the mill for export to New York City and beyond.*

Philip Van Cortlandt was among the commissioners. His sister, Cornelia Van Cortlandt Beekman, bought the manor house property and lived there for the rest of her life.

In the 1930s the property was threatened with destruction and subdivision into building lots. The Historical Society of the Tarrytowns enlisted the help of John D. Rockefeller, Jr. in financing its preservation. In 1940, Rockefeller purchased the property, which ultimately became part of Sleepy Hollow Restorations, and largely financed the restoration of the manor house. Philipsburg Manor Upper Mills, as it survives today, was once a part of one of the greatest commercial empires of colonial New York. Standing today are the restored manor house, an 18th-century barn brought to the site from another location in New York State, a water-powered gristmill recreated in the 1960s and a reconstructed tenant house. Also standing nearby is the original church, built in the 1680s by Philipse, who is buried in its crypt. The church was an important part of Philipsburg Manor, and still functions as The Old Dutch Church of Sleepy Hollow.

Although all of the Philipse family possessions were disbursed after the Revolution, a room by room probates inventory survived from 1750. This became the guide for refurbishing the manor house, undertaken largely in the 1960s and again in 2001. Today this collection of 17th- and 18th-century Dutch, English, and colonial American furnishings and household objects is one of the finest in the nation.

Kykuit

Kykuit is perhaps the most splendid of the houses built along the Hudson River, in that it demonstrates the successful integration of architecture, sculpture, garden design, and interior decoration. It was built by John D. Rockefeller, Sr., one of the great figures of the 19th century, who had made his fortune as the founder of the Standard Oil Company. Standard Oil was based in Cleveland, where Rockefeller and his family had a country house called Forest Hill. But in 1884, Rockefeller relocated to New York City and began to look for a suitable country property. In the summer of 1893, after much searching and careful planning, he bought 400 acres at Pocantico Hills in Westchester County, including a spot known as Kykuit (Dutch for lookout) with a splendid view of the Hudson River at the Tappan Zee, and the Palisades beyond.

The year 1893 brought great changes to American architecture. The World's Columbian Exposition, held in Chicago in 1892-93, with its brilliant white Classical architecture, signaled the demise of the picturesque styles. Led by McKim, Mead & White, Richard Morris Hunt, and Carrère & Hastings, the nation's foremost architects shifted away from the Romanesque and Queen Anne styles toward a more imperial manner, as represented on the Hudson River by Staatsburgh (1894) and Hyde Park (1896). Rockefeller's peers, such as Andrew Carnegie and the Vanderbilts no longer looked to 17th-century England for inspiration, but rather to ancient Rome and modern Paris.

Rockefeller was unmoved by these trends and did not rush to build a great house. Instead, he moved into one of several houses already on the site, a modest, mid-Victorian wood frame building called the Parsons-Wentworth house, and began to tinker with the design of the landscape, a matter of much greater interest to him than architecture. He engaged the Boston firm of Olmsted, Olmsted, and Eliot to prepare detailed plans for the estate. These included roads leading through a landscaped park to a proposed new house carefully located to maximize sunlight and views, on a newly leveled site on top of Kykuit Hill. At the same time, excavation began for the new house, and rock was set aside for its foundation.

Rockefeller had the frugality of the self-made millionaire and was disdainful of ostentation. His taste in architecture was modest. However, the final design of Kykuit was influenced less by Rockefeller and more by his son, JDR, Jr. The son graduated

from Brown University in 1897 and returned to New York to work in his father's office. He also managed the development of Kykuit on his father's behalf. Unlike the father, the son was born to great wealth, received a gentleman's education and, understandably, had a more developed taste for art and architecture. He found himself in a position of conflict, at once deferential to his father's goal of simplicity while firm in his determination to see that the new house and grounds achieved a measure of beauty and dignity that was suitable to his family's position.

JDR, Jr.'s first assignment, in 1899, was to engage the architecture firm York & Sawyer to design a new coach barn behind the Parsons-Wentworth house, to house the family's horses and carriages, maintenance facilities, and a boiler room for the estate. It was built of granite quarried from the house site, finished rustically in a manner in keeping with the building's use. The roof was clad in tile, steeply pitched and ornamented with brackets and dormers, and would prove influential to the eventual design of the main house.

In 1902 the Parsons-Wentworth house was destroyed by fire, causing father and son to accelerate their plans to build on Kykuit Hill. Rockefeller, Sr. commissioned designs from the architect Dunham Wheeler, but Wheeler worked in the Queen Anne style of the 1880s that JDR, Jr. considered inappropriate and old fashioned. On his own initiative he commissioned plans from his wife's distant cousin, Chester H. Aldrich, of Delano and Aldrich, a recently established New York architecture firm.

Designed by Codman, the library has an 18th-century English flavor reinforced by portraits by John Hoppner and Sir Thomas Lawrence. A portrait of George Washington by Gilbert Stuart, and another of Abraham Lincoln by Joseph Alexander Ames establish an aura for the room and the family. Tang Dynasty figures, a small sculpture by Auguste Rodin, and other objects were added by Happy and Nelson Rockefeller after 1960.

Four years went by, an interval that must have included much back and forth between father and son. But in 1906, JDR, Jr. prevailed, and Delano and Aldrich were given the commission. As young architects, they must have been overjoyed to receive such a prestigious assignment, but in the end it brought them nothing but disappointment. John D. Rockefeller, Sr. required them to use Wheeler's floor plan and many of his Queen Anne details, and to match the roof of the coach barn, this time much enlarged. As a final blow, the interior design was given over to the New York decorator Ogden Codman, Jr. When completed, the overall effect was a strange hybrid of influence, neo-classical details here, Queen Anne there. What was worse, the house made a less than satisfactory backdrop for the splendid neoclassical gardens designed under John D. Rockefeller Jr.'s direction by William Welles Bosworth.

Bosworth, born in 1869 in Marietta, Ohio, had an ideal apprenticeship for his work at Kykuit. He received his architectural training at the Massachusetts Institute of Technology, class of 1889, afterwards working for the great landscape architect, Frederick Law Olmsted. He further refined his training at the École des Beaux-Arts in Paris returning to New York to work for Carrère and Hastings, one of New York's great neoclassical firms, and architects of the New York Public Library. He opened his own practice, and in 1911 was commissioned by JDR, Jr. to build a town house on West 54th Street in New York, cementing a relationship that would last a lifetime. In 1906, when JDR, Jr. hired Bosworth to design the gardens at Kykuit, he was not well known and had done little work. But he had Rockefeller's trust, and it was that, and

The splendid Tea House (left) presides over the Inner Garden and overlooks the Morning Garden on the opposite side. Bosworth's decoration was inspired by Italian Renaissance precedent. The furniture, probably designed by Bosworth as well, was made by William Baumgarten & Co. in 1910. The vase in the corner was designed by Picasso. The forecourt (right, top) includes the monumental Oceanus group, made in Italy in 1913 after a 16th-century work in the gardens of the Pitti Palace in Florence. Gov. Nelson Rockefeller used the colonnade overlooking the rose garden (right, below) to frame Triangular Surface in Space, carved in granite in 1962 by Swiss artist Max Bill.

Bosworth's genius for both garden design and architecture that made Kykuit the success that it finally became.

By 1908 work was complete, and JDR, Jr. and his wife, Abby, moved into the house for six weeks to look after final preparations while his parents waited in Cleveland at Forest Hill. When they arrived and had their first look at the house, they were not pleased. Rockefeller's wife, Laura, was unhappy with the planning of the cramped rooms on the upper floors, tucked away as they were under the vast sloping roof. The service entrance was located under the master bedroom windows and disturbed her sleep. Rockefeller, for his part, was vexed by the downdraft in the chimneys that caused smoke to spew from the fireplaces.

John D. Rockefeller, Jr. must have been dismayed by his parents' disappointment, but he and Bosworth made the most of their opportunity. It was surely their prompting that led Rockefeller, Sr. to write to his son, "So desirous am I to have the chimneys right…that if it were not such tremendous trouble, I would be willing to run the walls of the house up higher, so that the main chimney could extend to the top of the roof."

Run the walls up they did. While Aldrich, the architect of record, looked on, Bosworth redesigned the house. The sweeping roof was removed and the walls built up to the full four stories. The garden was raised on the north front to cover the service entry and the wooden verandas removed and replaced with limestone colonnades. The entrance façade was rebuilt in a more suitable Classical style, with an elegant pediment, ornamented with sculpted allegorical figures. Tiffany designed bronze balconies, window grilles, and a magnificent metal and glass porte-cochere to replace the humble wooden one. The result was to transform Kykuit into a much more imposing house, one more complementary to Bosworth's gardens and Codman's interiors. Persuasive to the end, Bosworth convinced the Rockefellers to expand the forecourt and, as the final touch, add a colossal fountain modeled after Oceanus and the Three Rivers in the gardens of the Pitti Palace in Florence.

Rockefeller, Sr. finally moved into his house in 1913, twenty years after he purchased the land, and lived there until his death in 1937. JDR, Jr. followed up his triumph at Kykuit with numerous architectural and restoration projects, including the construction of the Cloisters and Rockefeller Center. He financed the formation and development of Colonial Williamsburg and founded Sleepy Hollow Restorations, the organization responsible for the restoration of Sunnyside, Philipsburg Manor and Van Cortlandt Manor. He lived at Kykuit until his death in 1960. Bosworth moved to France after World War I and became the architect for the restoration of Rheims Cathedral and the Palace of Versailles, projects financed by JDR, Jr. Ogden Codman moved to France too, where he built a great house for himself, called La Leopolda, and lived there until his death in 1951. Delano and Aldrich nursed their wounds after Kykuit, and went on to become New York's preeminent country house architects, practicing well into the 1950s.

The house is approached through one of two splendid iron gates into the walled forecourt (top), dominated by the Oceanus fountain. As is clearly evident, the house has magnificent views of the Hudson River and the Palisades. The effect is that the estate runs all the way to the river; in fact, the riverfront villages of Tarrytown and Sleepy Hollow intervene but are completely screened out by dense tree planting. Bosworth laid out the gardens (right) as a series of terraces and enclosed spaces, all different but interconnected and related to the formal arrangement of the rooms of the house. Gov. Nelson A. Rockefeller placed an important collection of 20th-century sculpture in the gardens, which includes works by Pablo Picasso, Henry Moore, Louise Nevelson, David Smith, Alexander Calder, Constantin Brancusi, Isamu Noguchi, and many others. He placed these works of art himself, often to brilliant effect. The original garden plan included a Japanese garden (lower right), rarely seen by visitors, which Gov. Rockefeller enthusiastically expanded and improved during his tenancy.

JDR, Jr.'s son, Gov. Nelson A. Rockefeller, occupied Kykuit from 1963 until 1979 and in his will left Kykuit and eighty-six acres of the estate to the National Trust for Historic Preservation. In 1991 an agreement was reached whereby the Rockefeller Brothers Fund would manage the Pocantico Historic Area, including Kykuit, its gardens and the coach barn, and Historic Hudson Valley would operate the property's visitors services and interpretation programs, allowing the public to visit Kykuit for the first time.

Lyndhurst

Bristling asymmetrically with turrets, crenellations and pinnacles, Lyndhurst is a superb example of Gothic Revival architecture. For his retirement home in the Hudson River Valley, William Paulding, Jr., hired the leading architect of the day, Alexander J. Davis. Davis's design for the house, originally called Knoll for the hillside overlooking the Hudson upon which it was built, broke from the traditional box-shaped mold to reflect, instead, the rugged, irregular landscape of the surrounding countryside. This new approach to architecture, which integrated the buildings with the land, was to have an enormous impact on the future of house design.

The Lyndhurst estate is emblematic of an era of great artistic, technological and political change in the United States. At the time the estate was being built, the country was struggling to come to terms with its national identity and to create a uniquely American culture. New York City had become the commercial and artistic center of the nation, and as New York grew, so did the desire of its wealthier inhabitants to build houses, to which they could escape on occasion, or pass the years of their retirement. Westchester was an ideal location for these houses. It was accessible by steamboat, and later by train, and the landscape was scenic, nowhere more so than alongside the Hudson River.

As New York grew wealthy, the arts flourished. In the 1820s and 1830s new ideas developed among a new generation of artists who were more worldly and sophisticated than those who came before. At the same time, the nearby Hudson River Valley changed from a quiet farming community to the locus of the Romantic Movement in painting, literature, architecture and landscape design. Some of the most important artists of the Romantic period were painters Thomas Cole, Frederick Church and Albert Bierstadt, authors Washington Irving and James Fenimore Cooper, and the architect Alexander Jackson Davis. These men comprised an artistic and intellectual community centered in New York City and the Hudson River Valley; they all knew one another and some even collaborated on projects. Davis studied art and worked as an architectural illustrator before becoming an architect. It was his ability to draw that enabled him to design so skillfully in many styles, including the Greek, Italianate and Gothic, and to become the foremost architect of his time. Lyndhurst, an outstanding villa overlooking the Tappan Zee from a bluff south of Tarrytown was Davis's masterpiece and is regarded as one of the best houses of the 19th century.

LEFT *The needs and tastes of the Merritt family were different from those of the Pauldings. They enlarged the house to nearly double its size and embellished the existing rooms to make them better reflect their new-found status. The once plain painted walls of the entry hall were now transformed with trompe l'oeil painting and marble tiles. The wheel-back oak chair and the marble busts (of George Washington and the Marquis de Lafayette), however, remain from the Paulding era. The chair, designed by Davis c. 1841, is one of the finest pieces in the house.*

RIGHT *What had been the rather small Paulding dining room now became the Merritt library. Today this room houses Gould's collection of books.*

BELOW *The Paulding library—once the masterpiece of the house—became the Merritts' picture gallery or billiard room seen here in this illustration of c. 1870. The change reflected not only the varying tastes of the families but also the changing times. By the 1860s the interests of the wealthy had shifted; the bibliophile was being replaced by the art collector.*

The oldest part of the house was built for William Paulding, Jr. and his son, Philip. The father was born in Tarrytown in 1770. He practiced law in New York, was elected to Congress in 1811, and was a brigadier general during the War of 1812. He was elected mayor of New York in 1824, lost the next election to Philip Hone, and was elected again in 1826. The Paulding family already had a house at Tarrytown, and had connections to Washington Irving, who lived nearby at Sunnyside. It was right after Irving renovated Sunnyside that the Pauldings decided to build a house on the 184 acres of land that they owned just to the north of Irving's house. In May of 1838, Davis visited the site for the first time, and in July, he prepared construction drawings for a new house, which the Pauldings called Knoll.

ABOVE *Once announced, a guest would proceed from the entrance hall to the reception room (above, c. 1870). The Italianate frescoes on the ceiling panels represent the hours of the day.*

OPPOSITE *While the library had been the finest room in the house under the Pauldings, the dining room became the Merritt family's showcase. Davis designed for them a room exuding opulence—faux marble columns, painted and stencilled wallcoverings, neoclassical marble statues, and thronelike chairs for the host and hostess.*

Davis was fortunate. Paulding was an intelligent client, with ambitious plans and a first-rate site. Davis designed him a house in the Gothic Revival style, with walls clad in Sing Sing marble, shaped and carved into a picturesque assortment of towers, gables, pinnacles and dormers, with a veranda wrapped around the south and west fronts. Paulding engaged Davis to prepare extensive details for the exterior stonework, kept him involved during construction, and had him design the stained glass windows, mantels, chairs and tables, in the interior. Davis had complete control of the design, and it was the unity of execution that made the final outcome such a rare success.

In 1864, Paulding's son Philip sold the house to George Merritt, a dry-goods merchant, who held a patent for a railroad car spring, an invention that brought him a handsome income. Merritt renamed the house Lyndenhurst, and decided to build a major addition, an alteration that, had it been designed by another architect, might have ruined it. Davis had already prepared a set of plans for an expansion, and perhaps for that reason Merritt hired him. To this building campaign belongs the five-story tower, and the handsome maroon and ochre dining room. Merritt's decorative requirements were much more elaborate than Paulding's had been and to compensate for this Merritt had Davis embellish most of the older rooms with new plaster trim and elaborate decorative finishes. Merritt commissioned Davis to design more furniture, sympathetic to the pieces Davis had designed for Paulding. Davis made the most of this final, unexpected opportunity to influence the architectural and decorative scheme of the house.

Merritt was a passionate horticulturist. He hired Ferdinand Mangold, once the superintendent of the gardens of King Leopold of Bavaria, to supervise improvements to the grounds. Mangold oversaw a crew of close to one hundred men, who drained the swamps, built roads, and planted trees and lawns, to create a handsome landscape. Merritt also had a huge greenhouse built, 390 feet long, topped with a metal and glass onion dome. When built, it was one of the largest privately owned greenhouses in the United States. Merritt lived at Lyndenhurst until his death in1873.

After the Civil War, Newport replaced the Hudson River Valley as the resort of choice for New York's elite. Davis and his picturesque architecture fell out of fashion, replaced by a new wave of architects, many of them trained in Paris, armed and ready with designs of ever-increasing sophistication. Davis continued his practice into the 1890s, but in an indication of the new times he built very little after his work for Merritt was completed in 1867. As fashions changed, many of his houses were altered beyond recognition and many more demolished.

In 1880, the financier Jay Gould bought the estate from the Merritt family, changed the name to Lyndhurst, and with his wife and six children used it as a retreat from their house on Fifth Avenue. Gould was a speculator and an investor, especially in railroads, and made a great fortune estimated at his death to be $77 million. But he made his fortune by methods considered ruthless, even by the lax standards of the time. Mrs. William Astor, the matriarch of New York society, refused to accept that the end might justify the means, and declined to count him among the "four hundred," her enumeration of society's inner circle. Many of that circle were members of the New York Yacht Club,

ABOVE The grounds of Lyndhurst, like the house, reflect the varying tastes and interests of the families that lived there. The first greenhouse on the property was built by George Merritt. It was one of the largest of its kind in the country and he filled it with exotic palms and rare plant specimens from around the world. This structure burned down in 1880 and Jay Gould built a new one on the site in the Gothic Revival style, uniting it aesthetically with the house. Only the skeleton of this structure remains today.

and they too denied Gould membership, despite his reputation as a yachtsman. It is hard to imagine a restless tycoon like Gould surrounded by the stately ribbed ceilings and stained glass at Tarrytown, but perhaps the social slights he had endured discouraged him from making the more fashionable choice of a gilded cottage in Newport. It may have been Gould's lack of interest, rather than admiration, which restrained him from altering Davis's masterwork. In the living room the furniture was replaced, new stained glass windows installed, and the walls and ceiling painted with stenciled patterns. Elsewhere, Gould was satisfied to change the floorboards and to hang his collection of European art, paintings by Corot, Courbet, Bouguereau, and others.

After Gould died in 1892, his daughter Helen lived on at Lyndhurst and bought the house from her siblings in 1898. She built many of the newer buildings on the property, including the bowling alley in 1894 (see inset), the kennels in 1897, a laundry building in 1911, an indoor swimming pool in 1913, and a little playhouse, called Rose Cottage, in 1916. She introduced a rose garden, in concentric circles around a central gazebo, just to the west of the greenhouses.

The last private owner of Lyndhurst was Helen Gould's younger sister Anna, Duchess of Tallyrand-Perigord. She had married in 1895 and moved to France, and after the death of her sister in 1938, returned to New York. She lived at the Plaza Hotel but made regular visits to Lyndhurst until 1961, when she returned to France. She died six months later, and in her will, left Lyndhurst to the National Trust for Historic Preservation, which operates it as a house museum, open to the public. Lyndhurst survives as a superb work of architecture and as an illustration of the great cultural and artistic history of the Hudson River Valley.

Washington Irving's
Sunnyside

Washington Irving was born in New York City on April 3, 1783, five months before the signing of the Treaty of Paris on September 3, and eight months before George Washington entered the city in triumph on December 4th. Irving and the nation grew up together, and he played a central role as New York became the nation's commercial and cultural center.

Irving achieved his early first success with the publication in 1809 of his *History of New York*, written under the pseudonym Diedrich Knickerbocker as a mythical account of New York's Dutch heritage. He followed this triumph with the publication in 1819 of *The Sketch Book*, which included the story of Rip Van Winkle, and won for himself both national and international acclaim. He led a peripatetic life, living after 1820 in Dresden, Paris, Bordeaux, and Madrid, writing numerous literary works, including *Life and Voyages of Columbus* (1828) and *The Conquest of Granada* (1829) and *The Alhambra* (1832). He returned to New York in 1832, and in 1835 purchased for $1,800 a small tenant farmhouse on land once part of the Manor of Philipsburgh, with the idea of transforming it into a Dutch-style cottage.

The tradition of the famous literary figure who builds a famous house was an English one, the first example of which is Horace Walpole, the son of Prime Minister Sir Robert Walpole, and the author of the first Gothic novel, *The Castle of Otranto*. In

1747, Walpole bought a small house in Twickenham, named it Strawberry Hill, and spent the rest of his life transforming it into a kind of Gothic novel in three dimensions. Walpole's follower, Sir Walter Scott, pioneer of the historical romance and hero to Irving, bought a small classical house in 1812, named it Abbotsford, and spent the rest of his life transforming it into a turreted Scottish castle. Irving had visited Sir Walter at his home and copied enough architectural details for use at Sunnyside to lead one to speculate that his initial intention was to build a miniature Abbotsford. But Abbotsford was created to illustrate Scott's literary connection to Scottish history, while Sunnyside, with its Dutch colonial flourishes, was meant to symbolize Irving's association with his mythology of old New Amsterdam.

Irving turned to his friend, the painter George Harvey (1800-1878), who had created his own picturesque cottage in nearby Hastings. It was Harvey who served as Irving's collaborator, as architect for the project and as overseer of the construction. Harvey sketched a watercolor of the old farmhouse for the record, and in 1835 he and Irving set about its complete transformation.

ABOVE *Because Washington Irving's study was sketched and described in detail by several people in the 1850s, it is one of the best documented period rooms in America. All of the furniture and most of the objects in this room are original. G. P. Putnam, Washington Irving's publisher, gave him the oak partner's desk in 1856.*

They replaced the clapboard gable ends with masonry, stepped in the traditional Dutch manner (or in the Scottish manner of Sir Walter Scott, take your pick). A little wing was added at the back with a porch overlooking the Hudson. The rough brick chimney top was removed and replaced with clustered chimney pots. Dormers were added and a coat of stucco applied over the masonry and scored, in the fashion of the period, to look like stone. As a final touch, Irving and Harvey added masonry tiebacks to the west façade, no doubt cosmetic, with ornamental iron numbers that announce the date of construction, as fictional as Irving's New York histories, of 1656.

Irving and Harvey's design was avant-garde in its time, built during the heyday of the Greek Revival. It was preceded by Davis's design for Glen Ellen, a Gothic Revival house in Maryland built for Robert Gilmore (Gilmore had visited Strawberry

Hill in 1830), but preceded Davis's masterpiece in Tarrytown, Lyndhurst, by three years. In 1835, Sunnyside's picturesque qualities were the exception rather than the rule, and it is this, as well as Harvey's and Irving's amateur status, that suggests that it be considered as a literary, rather than architectural, phenomenon.

Conscious that a picturesque house must sit in a picturesque landscape, Irving directed his attention to the grounds. He created a landscape with meandering pathways and artfully planned views of the Hudson River. A stone dam, with a small cascade, was built to create a landscape feature and to supply water to the house. Another pond was built, in a shady spot, to furnish ice in the wintertime. The less picturesque (but equally important) kitchen garden, stables, and hencoop were tucked away, along with the icehouse, on the north side of the house.

Irving moved into Sunnyside in 1836 and lived there until 1842, when President Tyler appointed him Minister to Spain. He returned in 1846, when he added the tower wing. During Irving's lifetime, Sunnyside was frequently illustrated and

OPPOSITE TOP AND BOTTOM *The kitchen was state-of-the-art in the mid 19th century. Conveniences include a cast-iron, wood-burning stove, gravity-fed running water, a hot water heater, cast-iron sink, built-in cabinets, storage pantry, and ice-box. Adjacent to the kitchen is a laundry fitted with built-in wash tubs. Irish-born servants kept house, cooked, and waited on table.*

ABOVE *The Sunnyside property lay like a giant circle with one edge touching the shore of the Hudson, one of a series of elegant villas lining the west bank of the Hudson by the mid-1800s. (Lyndhurst can be seen just to the north, or the Paulding property, Knoll, as it was then called). Sunnyside had beautifully laid-out gardens and the house received its water by gravity feed from the pond up the hill to the east, as can be seen in the photograph.*

RIGHT *The parlor opened out to a porch overlooking the Hudson River, just a stone's throw away. The handsome porch with its gothic detail was reconstructed in the restoration of the late 1950s.*

OPPOSITE *Washington Irving's bedroom, with its eclectic mix of furnishings, is located above his study. Irving died in this room on May 28, 1859, at the age of 76.*

RIGHT *The cozy bedroom was occupied by Washington Irving's nieces, Catherine and Sarah Irving, who served as the bachelor author's hostesses and inherited Sunnyside from their "Uncle Wash." The room contains a charming collection of their handiwork.*

BELOW *The first floor bathroom, with its zinc-lined tub, had hot running water.*

achieved an iconic fame that rivaled the author's own, not unlike that which Mt. Vernon achieved later in the century. It became known as a symbol not only of the author, but of American domestic life itself. In the 1850s Irving continued to live and write at Sunnyside, publishing a fanciful and fictionalized account of his house, *Wolfert's Roost*, and a five-volume biography of George Washington which he finished just before his death on May 28, 1859.

After Irving's death, his nieces, Catherine and Sarah Irving, inherited the property, and in 1896, his grandnephew Alexander Duer Irving built an enormous addition to the north, in the style of the original but nearly three times in size. The Irving family retained ownership until 1945, when John D. Rockefeller, Jr. purchased Sunnyside.

The house was opened to the public in 1947. As a mid-19th-century alteration of an 18th-century house, Sunnyside was unique at a time when interest in restoration was focused almost exclusively on the colonial period exemplified by the restoration work at Colonial Williamsburg. At the time, 19th-century architecture in the Romantic styles was not always admired, especially when created at the expense of an earlier, colonial specimen. However, Irving's and Sunnyside's place in American history and literature were indisputable and the primary reason for saving the property. In the 1950s the curators at Sunnyside made a decision to remove the 1896 addition and to restore the house to its condition during Washington Irving's lifetime.

Glenview

Charles Williams Clinton was the architect of Glenview, built between 1876 and 1877. Clinton was born in New York in 1838, was a descendant of George and DeWitt Clinton, both governors of New York, and was apprenticed at the age of sixteen to Richard Upjohn, the renowned architect of New York's Trinity Church. Clinton was one of a generation of architects who practiced in the years following the Civil War, designing buildings of ever-increasing scale and complexity. Working in a variety of colorful architectural styles, among them the Second Empire, Venetian Gothic, and Romanesque, and making use of the latest structural and mechanical innovations, they designed many of New York's early high-rise buildings. When fashions changed at the end of the 19th century, these buildings came to be seen as old-fashioned or worse, and often were badly treated. Many disappeared under the endless waves of commercial development in Manhattan.

Clinton designed Glenview early in his career as a country retreat for John Bond Trevor, a New York financier, and his family. The walls were built from local gray granite, trimmed with Ohio sandstone, the roof clad in various shades of slate and a copper cresting, all picturesquely massed and detailed in the mid-century Parisian manner of the architect Richard Morris Hunt. Glenview's materials, massing, arrangement of rooms and interior design may be compared to Hunt's famous Chateau-sur-Mer, the house he completed in the early 1870s in Newport, Rhode Island.

Glenview's twenty-four rooms were outfitted with the modern conveniences of indoor plumbing, gas lighting, and a huge coal-burning furnace. The decoration of the interior was in keeping with the latest fashion, the artistic interior of the Aesthetic Movement. Daniel Pabst, from Philadelphia, made the cabinetwork, and Leissner and Louis, from New York, painted the stenciled walls and ceilings. It is possible that Clinton collaborated with others on the interior design of the house, as this was not unusual at the time. Stanford White and Louis Comfort Tiffany designed some of the rooms in Clinton's Seventh Regiment Armory, on Park Avenue in New York.

The Aesthetic Movement, which was also known as Queen Anne, Arts and Crafts and Gothic Reform was an English phenomenon. In an article in the early 1880s, *Harper's* magazine noted that, "To Dante Rossetti, Burne-Jones, and William Morris do the lovers of artistic interiors owe an immortal debt, for they started in England a crusade against the bad features of household furnishing, which was born of the reign

of George the Fourth." These and other English reformers, including
Charles Locke Eastlake, advocated simple and restrained decoration,
and offered relief from the perceived heavy hand of the Victorian
Rococo Revival. It was Eastlake's best-selling 1868 book,
Hints on Household Taste, which initially popularized these
ideas in the United States.

The Centennial International Exhibition in
Philadelphia in 1876, like The World of Science, Art
and Industry in New York in 1853, and The World's
Columbian Exposition in Chicago in 1892-1893,
was well attended, and had a tremendous influence on American taste. Clinton exhibited his
work at the fair, and the Trevors' painting,
"Patrician Mother," by Anna Lea Merritt, won
a gold medal there. Among the many pavilions was one that *Harper's* magazine called a
"...pretty Eastlake house from England, with
its stuffs of all nations...picking out for us what
had been worthy in the reign of the tasteful
Stuarts, whatever was magnificent in the day of
stately Elizabeth, whatever of good (and there
was much) in the reign of Queen Anne." The
house, actually designed by the English architect
Thomas Harris, was wildly popular and did much to
encourage the adoption in America of the new English style. The Japanese and Chinese pavilions were
also popular and contributed to the growing interest in
orientalism, an important component of the Aesthetic
Movement and mid-century American design.

John Bond Trevor was born in Philadelphia in 1822, and
moved to New York in 1849, joined the New York Stock Exchange,
and formed the stock brokerage firm Trevor & Colgate. He was a successful businessman who had accumulated a large fortune. Trevor was president
of the Board of Trustees of the University of Rochester, and a benefactor of Colgate
University, the Rochester Theological Seminary, and the American Museum of
Natural History. Together with his partner and neighbor, James B. Colgate, he built
and presented to the congregation the Warburton Avenue Baptist Church in Yonkers
(destroyed in the 1970s). When Glenview was completed in 1877, Trevor had already
been living in Yonkers for fifteen years. Like many other well-to-do men of the era, he
had left Manhattan to find a more comfortable life for his family which, by 1871,
included his son Henry, his second wife, Emily Norwood, and their children, Mary,
Emily, and John, Jr.

John Trevor died in 1890. When Emily Trevor died in 1922, the trustees of the
estate put the property up for sale. By this time Yonkers had long since ceased to be a
haven for the rich, and the house was threatened with insensitive reuse or even demolition. Most of the house's contents were sold at auction in 1922 and Glenview itself
was sold at auction in 1923; fortunately, the City of Yonkers bought it and opened it in
1924 as the Yonkers Museum of Science and the Arts. (The museum was renamed
The Hudson River Museum at Yonkers in 1948, and in 1984 became The Hudson

ABOVE *The fairytale tiles under the mantel shelf are by Minton. The unusually large tile figure of Guinevere in the firebox is by Scottish artist Daniel Cottier, who opened a New York City branch of his London decorating firm in 1873.*

OPPOSITE *The Great Hall. Inspired by Eastlake's admiration of the furniture and architecture of the English Gothic period, Charles Clinton employed black walnut wainscoting and a "timbered" ceiling reminiscent of medieval great halls. Eastlake also advocated medieval-style encaustic tiles for their beauty and practicality as durable hall flooring.*

The Grand Staircase and laylight of the Great Hall (see also page 191) make it perhaps one of the finest surviving rooms of the Aesthetic Movement.

OPPOSITE *The Museum's collection of Kimbel & Cabus ebonized furniture is a highlight of the Library. The New York City firm was one of the first American companies influenced by Eastlake and displayed an ebonized parlor setting at the Centennial. The central chair, cabinet, and hanging shelf by the river window are all by Kimbel & Cabus. The circular bookcase, which belonged to the Trevor family, is similar in style.*

ABOVE *Notable features in the sitting room include original delicately incised bird's-eye maple cabinetry and French doors which led to the former side porch facing the Hudson River. The foreground chair, a patent recliner, belonged to Mr. Trevor.*

River Museum of Westchester). Many architectural details were altered or removed through the 1930s and despite intensive searches many of the original furnishings have never been located.In the late 1960s the museum began a program of restoration interpreting the house as a historic residence. The first period rooms opened in the 1970s. Recent restoration work, guided by original photographs and inventories, has focused on the completion of the major rooms on the first floor. These period rooms illustrate life during the Trevor years and allow the museum to display its own collection of decorative arts and paintings.

ABOVE *As part of the ambitious Glenview Restoration Campaign, skilled artists re-created the carved fireplace, stencils, field wallpaper and frieze based on a period photogravure from the mid 1880s, attributed to Edward Bierstadt. The blue enamel fireplace surround decorated with birds and the maple side chair in the bay window, both original to the room, also provided key evidence.*

LEFT *The billiard room which had been converted into a historical display gallery was completely restored in 1999. A period photograph of the Great Hall provided critical visual information for re-creating the woodwork in the billiard room. The color scheme comes from original paint samples in the billiard room bathroom. The fireplace, billiard table, and billiard light are period antiques from other residences.*

OPPOSITE *The stairs, with their exquisite sunflower carved banisters, echo a motif found throughout the house. The etched and painted laylight was uncovered during the recent restoration for the first time in more than thirty years. The gallery balustrade beneath the laylight is at the third floor level where the children and servants had their rooms.*

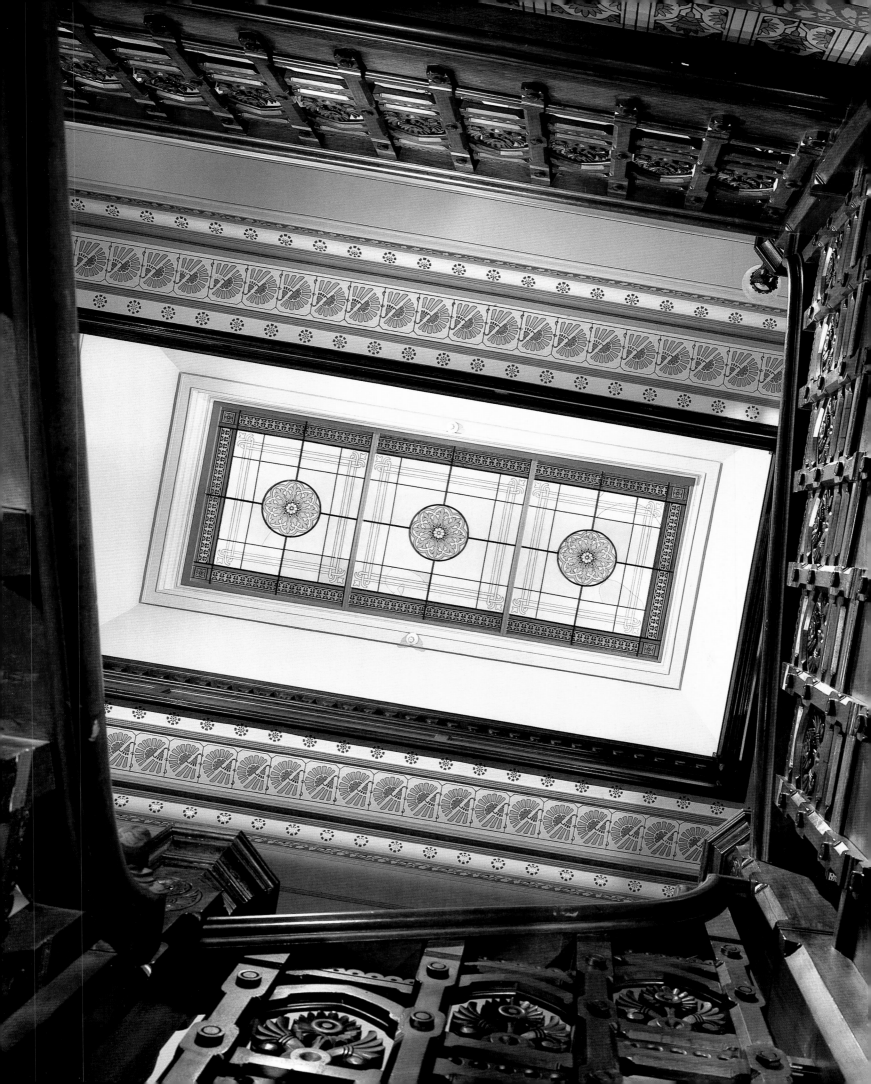

Philipse Manor Hall, the oldest house in southern Westchester County, was home to one of New York's wealthiest and most influential pre-Revolution families. Operated by the New York State Office of Parks, Recreation and Historic Preservation, the Manor Hall is the house around which the City of Yonkers grew and developed.

RIGHT Cast-iron fireback, 18th century. One of two at Philipse Manor Hall, this fireback depicts the coat of arms of Great Britain, a reminder of the Philipse family's staunch loyalism during the American Revolution.

Philipse Manor Hall

Philipse Manor Hall was built near the confluence of the Hudson and Saw Mill rivers. The Algonquian-speaking Lenape called the Hudson the Mahicanittuk or "the river that flows both ways," and called the Saw Mill the Neppehanuc. The Lenape had a summer fishing village there, called Neppeckamack or "fish trapping place." By 1640 they had begun to vacate their land as they were pushed out by the more aggressive Mohawk Indians who were trying to control the fur trade with the Dutch. These efforts were facilitated by their connections with a Dutchman named Adrian Van der Donck.

Van der Donck came from a rich Dutch family and was said to be the first lawyer to arrive in New Netherland. In 1645 he was instrumental in the negotiation of a treaty to settle disputes between the Mohawks, with whom he was then living, and the Dutch. For the services he rendered, the Dutch West India Company rewarded him with a "patroonship" in 1646, giving him authority over 24,000 acres of land just north of Manhattan. Adhering to Dutch custom, Van der Donck purchased the land from the remaining Lenape. The Saw Mill was a powerful river fueled by five waterfalls that cascaded down to the Hudson, and so it was natural that Van der Donck established, by 1649, a mill site there. He bore the title of *jonkheer* or "young gentleman" which meant he had considerable social standing, and because of this title, his land became known as "*jonkheer's* land," or Yonkers.

Van der Donck died in Holland in 1655, before he was able to complete the settlement of his colony, and Frederick Philipse, a carpenter from Amsterdam who became one of New York's richest merchants, eventually acquired Van der Donck's land. In the 1670s, Philipse began to purchase land along the Hudson River, beginning with the Yonkers mill site in 1672. Ultimately, his property included 52,000 acres, or about twenty-five percent of what is now called Westchester County. A Royal Patent in 1693 confirmed the title and established the estate as the Manor of Philipsburg. Philipse was no doubt attracted to the Yonkers mill site because of the potential for profit in the flour trade. He built gristmills and used sloops to transport flour down the Hudson to wharves owned by his family in New York City, and probably built the earliest part of Philipse Manor Hall by 1680. Philipse also established a site called the Upper Mills, on the northern part of the estate at the Pocantico River. Slaves largely operated the mill sites on the manor, and records from 1751 show there were approximately forty-one at the two mill sites. Of those, eighteen worked at the Yonkers site, including farmers, boatmen, millers, and house servants. As Lord of the Manor, Frederick Philipse collected rent from tenant farmers, who leased their land from him on a lifetime basis.

When Frederick Philipse died in 1702, Philipsburg Manor was divided. To his adopted daughter Eva Van Cortlandt he gave a large farm in the eastern portion, land that is today Van Cortlandt Park. To his son Adolph he gave the Upper Mills, and to his grandson Frederick Philipse II he gave the Lower Mills, along with the hereditary title of Lord of the Manor. The grandson was born in Barbados, the son of Adolph's older brother. In 1702 he was seven years old and an orphan, and was put in the care of his grandfather's second wife, Catherine Van Cortlandt. She had him educated in the English tradition, and saw that the Dutch carpenter's grandson became a proper English gentleman, made a good marriage to Lieutenant Governor Brockholl's daughter and took his place among the Philipse family enterprise and the established elite of New York. While maintaining his family's mercantile interests, Frederick II pursued a career in law and politics. He became an Alderman, a Justice of the Peace, Speaker of the Provincial Assembly and Provincial Treasurer. In 1755 he was appointed Second Judge of the New York Supreme Court. A devout Anglican, he donated funds to build St. John's Episcopal Church in Yonkers, and was said to be responsible for the design of Bowling Green in Manhattan, New York City's first public park. Frederick Philipse II's primary residence was in New York City. However, he enlarged the Manor Hall in the 1740s and transformed it from a small commercial outpost into a proper English country house. Such a house was rare at that time in the countryside along the Hudson River. It would have had only one rival—Robert Livingston's Clermont, built around 1750.

TOP *Philipse Manor Hall as it appeared c. 1850. After the Philipse family was forced to flee at the end of the American Revolution, the Manor Hall became home to a series of wealthy Yonkers residents, among them Lemuel Wells and William Woodworth.*

Adolph Philipse died in 1750, and Frederick Philipse II died the following year. His eldest son, Frederick Philipse III, became the third Lord of the Manor and owner of both the Upper and Lower mill sites. Colonel Philipse, as he was known, had little interest in trade and politics and was more inclined toward the study of literature and the cultivation of his exquisite Rococo garden. In a break with tradition, he and his family lived year-round at the Manor Hall, sufficiently supported by family investments and manor rents. As a man of refined tastes, Philipse made his Yonkers house a showcase of English architectural style. He renovated parts of the interior to conform to current English fashion, with elaborate Georgian woodwork and paneling and installed magnificent papier-mâché Rococo ornaments to the ceiling of the drawing room, with cameo medallions of Alexander Pope and Sir Isaac Newton.

ABOVE *Philipse Manor Hall decorated in mourning for President William McKinley, 1901. The Manor Hall became Yonkers Village Hall in 1868, and in 1872 Yonkers' first City Hall. During its tenure as the municipal center, the property was the logical choice for the location of the Soldiers' and Sailors' monument, dedicated in 1891 to those Yonkers residents who fought in the American Civil War.*

During the American Revolution, Frederick Philipse III declared his allegiance to the English Crown and fled with his family to British-occupied New York City. In 1779 the New York State legislature declared him and several other loyalists to be felons, to be punished by death if caught. The Manor of Philipsburg was dissolved, the land confiscated and sold at auction, and at the end of the war, in 1783, the family fled to England. The last Lord of Philipsburg Manor was buried in 1786 at Chester Cathedral in Chester, England.

In 1868, Philipse Manor Hall became the Village Hall, and later the City Hall, of Yonkers, but by 1903 the city government had outgrown these quarters. A proposal to enlarge the old building brought outraged protests from preservationists, and in 1908, Eva Smith Cochran, heiress to a Yonkers carpet mill fortune, donated funds to allow

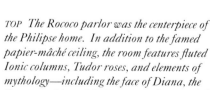

TOP *The Rococo parlor was the centerpiece of the Philipse home. In addition to the famed papier-mâché ceiling, the room features fluted Ionic columns, Tudor roses, and elements of mythology—including the face of Diana, the Roman goddess of the hunt, over the mantelpiece. The ceiling has been described as the finest work of its kind in North America, unique in that it is both in situ and open to the public.*

ABOVE RIGHT *Second floor parlor. Identical in size and shape to the Rococo parlor below, this somewhat less ornate chamber contains elements (on either side of the overmantel) that were copied in its downstairs counterpart. This room, in a slightly modified form, also served as the City Clerk's office.*

INSET *Medallion, from the Rococo ceiling. Poet Sir Alexander Pope and physicist Sir Isaac Newton, two framers of the Rococo movement, make up a dyad of recognizable personages in a ceiling that features game birds, hunting dogs, musicians and idealized elements of the natural world outside the Manor Hall. The ceiling, made of papier-mâché forms attached to a plaster ceiling, was installed by Frederick Philipse III in the mid-18th century.*

ABOVE *East entrance. Somewhat of a non-sequitur, these imported Dutch doors contrast strongly with the high-style Georgian architecture that surrounds the house's exterior. The Philipse family, although Loyalist by affiliation, were Dutch by ancestry and had at least one set of Dutch doors brought to the New World in the 18th century as a reminder of their homeland.*

RIGHT *South staircase. This view is taken from the remaining section of the third floor, which was home to children, slaves, and domestic servants.*

OPPOSITE *The Gothic Chamber. The Village government, upon taking up residency in the Manor Hall in 1868, made a conscious decision to preserve the historic fabric of the house intact. The one major exception was this room, where clearing away the walls and ceiling made way for the City Council's meeting room. Ornate American Gothic tracery contributes to the room's cathedralesque atmosphere.*

INSET PORTRAITS *The Manor Hall has been used as a museum since its preservation as a state historic site. All the Philipse furniture which was not taken to England with the family was sold at auction and consequently the Hall has been empty of original furniture since the 18th century. In 1912 Alexander Smith Cochran sought to embellish the Hall and create a museum imbued with historic and patriotic interest by purchasing seventy portraits by American artists of American presidents. military heros, statesmen, and educators. Entitled the Cochran Collection of American Portraiture, the collection contains one of five national collections on American presidents from George Washington to Calvin Coolidge. Cochran left the collection to the state in his will in 1929 for continued exhibition. Pictured here are portraits of George Washington, Andrew Jackson, Abraham Lincoln, and Martin Van Buren, from the collection.*

New York State to buy the house. On April 27, 1908, a bill was signed into law by the New York State Legislature authorizing an expenditure of $50,000 for the purchase of Philipse Manor Hall, committing it to the custody of the American Scenic and Historic Preservation Society. The manor house was thus "preserved and maintained forever intact as a historic monument and a museum of historic relics and patriotic uses."

In 1912 Eva Cochran's son, Alexander Smith Cochran, sought to create a museum with historic and patriotic interest by purchasing 70 portraits by American artists of American presidents, military heroes, statesmen, and educators. Entitled the Cochran Collection of American Portraiture, it includes one of five national collections of presidential portraits, from George Washington to Calvin Coolidge. In his will in 1929, Cochran left this collection to the state for exhibition at Philipse Manor Hall.

In 1924 the State Council of Parks was founded and historic sites in New York State were placed under its jurisdiction. In 1981, this agency became the Office of Parks, Recreation and Historic Preservation, which continues to operate Philipse Manor Hall as a New York State Historic Site.

Wave Hill

In 1646 the Dutch West India Company granted a large parcel of land in New York to a certain Adrian van der Donck in return for services rendered. The land included the area now known as Riverdale in the Bronx and Yonkers in Westchester. Van der Donck's almost feudal title included the right to hunt, to build houses of worship, administer justice and, very importantly, to bequeath the land in his will.

ABOVE *This 1912 view looks southwest, over the grass roof of the recreation building with its balustrade; (top) almost the same view today.*

When the English defeated the Dutch in 1664, they allowed van der Donck's widow to retain his rights although the patroonship was later divided and sold. One of the purchasers was Frederick Philipse: assembling other parcels from the 1670s on, in 1693 he received a Royal Patent that established "the lordship and manor of Philipse-borough," extending from Spuyten Duyvil Creek all the way to the Croton River. The manor passed through two generations to Frederick Philipse III. A Loyalist, at the end of the Revolutionary War he fled to England. His land was confiscated and sold by the Commissioners of Forfeiture. Many former tenants bought the land, now available freehold, including two local farmers, George and William Hadley. In the 1790s, they sold the land to William Ackerman and John Vestervelt. In 1836 Ackerman's heirs sold a parcel of fifteen acres to a New York attorney William Lewis Morris which became the property now known as Wave Hill.

INSET LEFT Appleton rebuilt and enlarged the original Morris house and renamed it Holbrook Hall. This c.1869 view shows the addition of a fashionable mansard roof in the French Second Empire style, surmounted by a small rectangular conservatory. The new porch with its Ionic columns faced the Hudson River.

INSET FAR LEFT A 1937 Christmas card of Wave Hill House rebuilt to the designs of Boston architects Putnam and Cox for George W. Perkins' daughter, Dorothy, her husband, Edward Woolsey Freeman, and their five children. Note the service roads, paths, and vegetable and cutting gardens on the west slope behind the house.

Morris was born to a prominent New York family. In 1662 his ancestor, Richard Morris, had settled on 2000 acres in the southeast Bronx, an estate known as Morrisania. Richard's great-grandson, Lewis Morris, Jr., was a signer of the Declaration of Independence for New York State. After the Revolutionary War, New York City grew rapidly and was the largest in the nation by 1836. Crowding and poor sanitation resulted in several cholera epidemics. Well-to-do New Yorkers had for years escaped these conditions and built houses in what was then the countryside of upper Manhattan. Although the crash of 1837 forestalled Morris's building plans, in 1843 he, his wife Mary Elizabeth Babcock, and their seven children were able to move into

ABOVE *Wave Hill from the west. Five copper beeches,* Fagus sylvatica *'atropurpurea,' were planted in the Appleton era. Their smooth gray trunks bear the mark of grafting, the only technique available a century ago to ensure duplication of the red leaf color.*

their two-story Greek Revival house built from local gray fieldstone, with a porch framed by Ionic columns. A sketch of it appeared in William Wade's *Panorama of the Hudson*. Numerous other houses were built in the following years such as Stonehurst to the north in 1852 and Parkside and Nonesuch to the south. The latter were part of a planned suburban development called Park-Riverdale, a part of which was a five-acre parcel on the river set aside for "ornamental pleasure grounds and walks."

Morris lived at Wave Hill with his family from 1843-1851. He died in 1864 and his heirs sold Wave Hill to a publishing scion, William Henry Appleton. Appleton remodeled the house in 1866-1869, adding a third floor with a mansard roof in the Second Empire style. He built a greenhouse, stables, and new wing in 1890, this time in the Romanesque style of the architect Henry Hobson Richardson. Among his famous guests were Thomas Huxley and Charles Darwin. Huxley declared the Palisades, which he could see across the river, one of the world's greatest natural wonders. From time to time, Appleton leased the house, which he called Holbrook Hall. In the summers of 1870-1871, Theodore Roosevelt rented it for his family. Appleton died in 1899 and his family rented the house again in 1901-1903, this time to Mark Twain.

TOP, ABOVE, AND TOP RIGHT
Armor Hall was added to Wave Hill House in 1927 by Bashford Dean explicitly to display his world-renowned collection of armor. After his death, many of the objects were accessioned by the Metropolitan Museum of Art. The architectural details include a Musician's Gallery, often a feature in medieval great halls.

In 1903 Wave Hill was purchased by George Walbridge Perkins, a partner in J. P. Morgan. Prior to this, Perkins had bought a number of the surrounding villas, including Nonesuch, where he lived with his family. Perkins commissioned the architect C. Grant La Farge to remodel and enlarge Nonesuch and renamed it Glyndor. Perkins's estate manager, Albert Millard, had been trained as a gardener at the Royal Garden in Vienna, and together they designed the terraces that are the foundation for the gardens at Wave Hill today. A Palm House and more greenhouses were added in 1906, designed by Lord and Burnham. He hired another architect, Robert M. Byers, to build an outdoor swimming pool and a recreational facility, with a bowling alley, squash court, and a billiard room, all tucked discretely under the garden. A tunnel lined with Guastavino tiles led back to Glyndor. The land was graded and contoured, the gardens planted to enhance the spectacular natural beauty of the Hudson River. In 1926 a bolt of lightning did such damage to the house that it was torn down and replaced by the house currently on the site, designed by architects Butler and Corse.

By 1911 Perkins owned eighty acres and numerous houses in the area. His

ABOVE *The fireplace in Armor Hall has 15th-century Spanish Gothic capitals and a three-quarter round bas-relief of the Resurrection that is possibly unique. Traditional in its design, with the male and female donors flanking the main scene, what is unusual is the garb of the four guards. They are all in suits of armor. Three are asleep, one with his visor down. The fourth looks at the strong vertical figure of the risen Christ in the center of the composition. Even the guards' pikes are medieval in form.*

TOP *The retaining wall, with its garden shed, supports the Great Lawn and pergola overlooking the Hudson River. (The full extent of the massive sixty-yard wall can be seen in the aerial photograph on pages 200-201).*

ABOVE *Architecturally the most interesting building on the Wave Hill property, this view from the northwest shows the underground recreation building with its lawn roof and balustrade. When it was built it served a second purpose, to thwart the imposition of New York City's angular grid street plan on Riverdale's meandering country lanes.*

CENTER LEFT *The Adirondack-style fireplace in the recreation building. Two stories below grade, the building contained a bowling alley, squash court, playroom, servants' quarters and workshops. The murals above the bowling alley show Hopi life and are attributed to Frederick Samuel Dellenbaugh.*

LEFT *Appleton engaged architects Babb, Cook and Willard for a second enlargement of Wave Hill. The work was executed between January and June 1890. A room was designed by Lockwood de Forest, who supplied this teak wood mantel carved in his Indian workshops. The colorful glazed tiles were purchased by de Forest as antiques in Damascus.*

In keeping with the tradition of estate gardens, unusual ornamental trees have been planted. Idesia polycarpa is an example. A native of China, it is dioecious, meaning that a male and female of the species must be planted together to produce the glorious red garnish which remains vibrant throughout the winter.

property stretched west from what is now Riverdale Avenue to the Hudson River and north from Spaulding's Lane to 254th Street. He leased most of the houses including Wave Hill whose long-term tenant was Bashford Dean. Dean was Professor of Zoology at Columbia University, Curator of Reptiles and Fishes at the American Museum of Natural History, and Curator of Arms and Armor at the Metropolitan Museum of Art. His collection of armor was internationally renowned and in 1927 he had a wing added to Wave Hill to house it, designed by a local architect, Dwight James Baum.

Perkins retired from J. P. Morgan in 1910 and until his death in 1920 devoted himself to philanthropic activities. He and his friend and former Wave Hill tenant Theodore Roosevelt founded the Progressive Party. At Roosevelt's urging, Perkins became the founding chairman of the Palisades Interstate Park Commission, formed to protect the Palisades on the New Jersey side of the Hudson. The Commission later became a model for the National Parks system.

In 1933 Perkins's daughter, Dorothy, her husband Edward Woolsey Freeman and family, moved into Wave Hill House. They commissioned the Boston firm of Putnam and Cox to redesign the house in a Georgian Revival makeover which is the present house. The Freemans too, rented the house: Arturo Toscanini lived there from 1942-1945, and the chief British delegates to the United Nations, Sir Gladwyn Jeff and Sir Pierson Dixon

from 1950-1956. The Queen Mother visited during their tenancy.

In 1960, the Perkins-Freeman families deeded Wave Hill to the City of New York. It is one of thirty-four City-owned cultural institutions. Wave Hill Inc, formed in 1965, is a nonprofit organization with an independent Board of Trustees responsible for managing the place. Today Wave Hill offers programs in the sciences, horticulture, environmental education, landscape history, visual, performing and literary arts, all designed to foster public appreciation for the sustaining nature of environmental relationships. Wave Hill Inc. maintains the gardens and greenhouses and manages a ten-acre urban woodland, providing an oasis of serenity within the city of New York.

A Guide to the Houses

in order of appearance:

Schuyler Mansion

A New York State Historic Site
New York State Office of Parks,
Recreation and Historic Preservation
32 Catherine Street
Albany, NY 12202
Tel: 518.434.0834 Fax: 518.434.3821
Internet: www.nysparks.com/hist
OPEN: Mid-April through Oct., Wed.–Sat
10–5pm; Sun. 1–5. Call for winter hours.
Group tours by reservation only; available year
round.
DIRECTIONS: *From North*: 1-87 to exit 7
(Troy) to I-787 South (Albany). Exit 3B
(Madison Avenue). At third light, left onto
South Pearl Street. At second light, right onto
Morton Ave; fourth left onto Elizabeth Street;
first immediate left onto Catherine Street.
From South: 1-87 to exit 23 to I-787 North to
exit 2 (Port of Albany.) Take left then bear
right to Rt. 32 North (Greene St.) At third light
left onto Rensselaer Street. Fourth left onto
Clinton Street; first immediate left onto
Catherine Street.

Luykas Van Alen House

A National Historic Landmark (1968)
Columbia County Historical Society
5 Albany Avenue (PO Box 311)
Kinderhook, NY 12106
Tel: 518.758.9265 Fax: 518.758.2499
Internet: www.berk.com/cchs
OPEN: Memorial Day through Labor Day,
Thurs.–Sat., 11–5pm; Sun. 1-5pm. Group tours
by appt. only.
DIRECTIONS: On Rt. 9H just south of
Kinderhook.

Lindenwald

A National Historic Landmark (1961)
Martin Van Buren National Historic Site
National Park Service, Dept. of the Interior
1013 Old Post Road
Kinderhook, NY 12106
Tel: 518.758.9689 Fax: 518.758.6986
Internet: www.nps.gov/mava
OPEN: Mid-May through Oct., daily,
9–4.30pm; Nov.–Dec. 5 weekends only.
DIRECTIONS: On Rt. 9H just south of
Kinderhook.

Bronck Museum

A National Historic Landmark
Greene County Historical Society
90 County Rt. 42
Coxsackie, NY 12051
Tel: 518.731.6490 Fax: 518.731.7672
Internet: www.gchistory.org/
OPEN: For guided tours. Memorial Day
weekend to October 15, Tues.–Sat. and Mon.
holidays 10–4pm; Sun. 1–5pm.
DIRECTIONS: From exit 21B on I-87 go
south 3.75 miles on Rt. 9W. Then right onto
Pieter Bronck Road.

Olana

A National Historic Landmark (1965)
New York State Office of Parks, Recreation
and Historic Preservation
5720 State Rt. 9G
Hudson, NY 12534
Tel: 518.828.0135   Fax: 518.828.6742
Internet: Olana.org
OPEN: April through Oct., Wed.–Sat.,
10–4pm. (Visitor Center and Museum Shop
9:30–4.30pm.)
DIRECTIONS: *From north*: Entrance off Rt.
9G, 1 mile south of the Rip van Winkle Bridge.
From south: 5 miles north of the traffic light in
Germantown on Rt. 9G.

Clermont

A National Historic Landmark (1973)
A New York State Historic Site
New York State Office of Parks,
Recreation and Historic Preservation
One Clermont Avenue
Germantown, NY 12526
Tel: 518.537.4240 or 518.537.TOUR
Fax: 518.537.6240
Internet: www.friendsofclermont.org
OPEN April–October: Tues. through Mon.
and holidays, 11am-5pm; last tour at 4.30.
Nov.–mid-Dec.: weekends. 11-4pm.
DIRECTIONS : Entrance off Rt. 9G, 7.9
miles north of the intersection of Rt. 9G and
Rt. 199, near the approach to the Kingston-
Rhinecliff Bridge.

Blithewood

Annandale-on-Hudson, NY 12504
OPEN: Not open to the public.

Montgomery Place

A National Historic Landmark (1992)
A property of Historic Hudson Valley
150 White Plains Road
Tarrytown, NY 10591
Estate located on River Road ,
Annandale-on-Hudson, NY 12504
Tel: 914.758.5461 Fax: 914.758.0545
Internet: www.hudsonvalley.org
OPEN: April-Oct: daily except Tues.
Weekends: Nov.–mid-Dec.
DIRECTIONS: Located in the hamlet of
Annandale-on-Hudson. Entrance off Rt. 9G,
2.9 miles north of the intersection of Rt.9G
and Rt. 199, near the approach to the
Kingston-Rhinecliff Bridge.

Edgewater

OPEN: Not open to the public.

Wilderstein

National Register of Historic Places
Wilderstein Preservation
330 Morton Road (PO Box 383)
Rhinebeck, NY 12572
Tel: 845.876.4818   Fax: 845.876.3336
Internet: www.wilderstein.org
OPEN: May through Oct., noon–4pm. (Last
tour 3:30.); Dec. on weekends – call to confirm.
DIRECTIONS: From the center of
Rhinebeck village drive 1/2 mile south on Rt.
9. Right onto Mill Road. Drive 2.2 miles then
right onto Morton Road. 1/4 mile to entrance.

Staatsburgh

New York State Office of Parks, Recreation and Historic Preservation
PO Box 308, Staatsburg, NY 12580
Tel: 845.889.8851   Fax: 845.889.8321
Internet: www.nyspark.state.ny.us
OPEN: April–Labor Day: Wed–Sat 10–5pm; Sun 12-5pm. Labor Day–Oct: Wed–Sun 12-5pm. Special Christmas hours. Please call for other times.
DIRECTIONS: *From north*: from the center of Rhinebeck go south 4.6 miles on Rt. 9 to Old Post Road. Go 0.9 miles to estate entrance. *From south*: On Rt. 9 go north through Hyde Park and 3.3 miles past the entrance to the Vanderbilt Mansion. Take Old Post Road 1.3 miles to estate entrance.

Hyde Park: The Vanderbilt Mansion

A National Historic Landmark (1940)
National Park Service:
Vanderbilt Mansion National Historic Site
Hyde Park, NY 12538
Tel: 845.229.9115   Fax: 845.229.0739
Internet: www.nps.gov/VAMA
OPEN: Daily, year-round. 9-5pm
DIRECTIONS: Entrance on Rt. 9 at the north end of the village of Hyde Park.

Springwood

A National Historic Landmark (1944)
National Park Service: Home of Franklin Delano Roosevelt National Historic Site
Hyde Park, NY 12538
Tel: 845.229.9115   Fax: 845.229.0739
Internet: www.nps.gov
OPEN: Daily, year-round. 9-5pm
DIRECTIONS: Entrance on Rt. 9 at the south end of the village of Hyde Park.

Val-Kill

A National Historic Landmark (1977)
Eleanor Roosevelt National Historic Site
Hyde Park, NY 12538
Tel: 845.229.9115   Fax: 845.229.0739
OPEN: May–Oct., daily, 9-5pm; Nov.–April: weekends only 9–5pm.
DIRECTIONS: Entrance on Rt. 9G, north of the intersection with St. Andrews Road.

Top Cottage

A National Historic Landmark (1997)
Hyde Park, NY 12538
Tel: 845.229.9115   Fax: 845.229.0739
Internet: www.nps.gov
OPEN: May–Oct., Thurs.–Mon. Limited tours starting form Springwood (see above.)
DIRECTIONS: There is a shuttle bus tour available from Springwood (see above.)

Locust Grove

The Samuel Morse Historic Site
A National Historic Landmark (1964)
2683 South Road (Rt. 9)
Poughkeepsie, NY 12601
Tel: 854.454.4500   Fax: 845.485.7122
Internet: www.morsehistoricsite.org
OPEN: House: daily May to Thanksgiving.; all bus and group tours by reservation only (call). Grounds: year-round, 8am–dusk weather permitting. Morse Gallery and museum shop open year-round 10–5pm.
DIRECTIONS: Entrance on Rt. 9 in Pough-keepsie, 2 miles south of the Mid-Hudson Bridge (Rt.s 44/55) or 11 miles north of I-84.

Madam Brett Homestead

50 Van Nydeck Avenue
Beacon, NY 12508
Tel: 845.831.6533
Internet: www.geocities/melzingah/
OPEN: By appointment only for group or private tours
DIRECTIONS: from North: Exit 11 off I-84, south on Rt. 9d to first light. Left onto Verplank Ave. to second light. Right onto Fishkill Ave., through next light (Main St) to Van Nydeck Ave. From south: Rt. 9D North into Beacon, right onto Teller Ave. Van Nydeck Ave. is the fourth street on the right.

Boscobel

National Register of Historic Places (1977)
Boscobel Restoration, Inc.
1601 Route 9D
Garrison, NY 10524
Tel: 845.265.3638   Fax: 845.265.4405
Internet: www.boscobel.org
OPEN: Closed Tuesdays, Thanksgiving and Christmas Day. April through Oct: 9:30–5pm (last tour at 4:15pm); Nov. and Dec: 9:30–4pm (last tour at 3:15pm).
DIRECTIONS: 1 mile south of the intersection of Rts. 9D and 301 in Cold Spring.

Van Cortlandt Manor

A National Historic Landmark
A property of Historic Hudson Valley
150 White Plains Road
Tarrytown, NY 10591
Tel: 914.631.8200 Fax: 914.631.0089
Internet: www.hudsonvalley.org
OPEN: April–Dec., daily except Tues.
DIRECTIONS: From Rt. 9 take the Croton Point exit. Van Cortlandt Manor is at the end of South Riverside Avenue, Croton-on-Hudson.

Philipsburg Manor

A National Historic Landmark
A property of Historic Hudson Valley
150 White Plains Road
Tarrytown, NY 10591
Tel: 914.631.8200 Fax: 914.631.0089
Internet: www.hudsonvalley.org
OPEN: March-Dec., daily except Tues.
DIRECTIONS: Turn left on Route 9N in Sleepy Hollow, NY about 2 miles north of the Tappan Zee Bridge, Tarrytown, NY.

Kykuit

The Rockefeller Estate
A National Historic Landmark
A historic site of the National Trust, operated and maintained by the Rockefeller Brothers Fund; Historic Hudson Valley operates the public program.
Historic Hudson Valley
150 White Plains Road
Tarrytown, NY 10591
Tel: 914.631.9491 Fax: 914.631.0089
Internet: www.hudsonvalley.org
OPEN: May through Nov. 1. Tours begin at 9:30am; last tour 4.45pm.
DIRECTIONS: Tours start at the Kykuit Visitor Center at Philipsburg Manor. Take I-87 to exit 9 (last exit before the Tappan Zee Bridge). Go 2 miles north on Rt. 9. Also accessible via Metro North (Tarrytown Station).

Lyndhurst

A National Trust Historic Site
635 South Broadway
Tarrytown, NY 10591
Tel: 914.631.4481 Fax: 914.631.5634
Internet: www.lyndhurst.org
OPEN: Mid-April through Oct., Tues–Sun and holiday Mon., 10–5pm (last tour 4:15); Nov. through mid-April, weekends and holiday Mon. only, 10–4pm (last tour at 3:30.)
DIRECTIONS: Take I-87 to exit 9 (last exit before the Tappan Zee Bridge). Go south on Rt. 9 1/2 mile. Entrance is on the right.

Sunnyside

A National Historic Landmark
A property of Historic Hudson Valley
150 White Plains Road
Tarrytown, NY 10591
Tel: 914.631.8200 Fax: 914.631.0089
Internet: www.hudsonvalley.org
OPEN: March weekends; April-Dec., daily except Tues.
DIRECTIONS: End of West Sunnyside Lane, off Route 9, about a mile south of the Tappan Zee Bridge, Tarrytown, NY.

Glenview

National Register of Historic Places (1977)
The Hudson River Museum
511 Warburton Avenue
Yonkers, NY 10701
Tel: 914.963.4550   Fax: 914.963.8558
Internet: www.hrm.org
OPEN: May through Sept, Wed–Sun. 12-5pm,
Fri. 12–9pm; Oct.–April, Wed–Sun 12-5pm.
DIRECTIONS: *North or South.* Take Saw Mill
Parkway to exit 9 (Executive Bvld). Go straight
and follow to end. Left onto Broadway. Next
right–Odell Avenue–to end. Left onto
Warburton Avenue. Go 1.3 miles. Museum is
on right.

Philipse Manor Hall

A New York State Historic Site
New York State Office of Parks,
Recreation and the Environment
29 Warburton Avenue (at Dock Street)
PO Box 496, Yonkers, NY 10702
Tel: 914.965.4027   Fax: 914.965.6485
Internet: www.nysparks.com or
www.philipsemanorfriends.org
OPEN : April through Oct., Wed. through Sat.,
12–5 pm; Sun., 1–4pm. Tours are on the hour
each hour. (Last tour 1 hr before closing).
Group tours by appt. year-round.
DIRECTIONS Exit 5 from Saw Mill Parkway
(Yonkers Ave.). Go west 1 1/4 miles; right onto
Riverdale Ave., after third light entrance is on
left. By Metro-North: to Yonkers Station.
PMH is two blocks east.

Wave Hill

West 249th Street and Independence Avenue
Tel: 718.549.3200   Fax: 718.884.8952
Internet: www.wavehill.org
OPEN: April 15–Oct.4, daily, 9–5:30pm; Oct.
15–April 14, 9–4.30. Until sunset on wed. in
June and July.
DIRECTIONS: *From South (West side):* Exit 21
(226-250th St.) off Henry Hudson Parkway,
north to 252nd St, left at overpass, left again,
right at 249th St. to gate. *From South (East
side):* Exit 12 off Major Deegan, first right to
Henry Hudson Parkway (south), exit 22 (254th
St.), left at stop sign, left at light, right at 249th
St. to gate. *From North :* same as for *From South
(East side)* from Henry Hudson Parkway. *By
train:* MetroNorth to Riverdale. (call for map).

Photo Credits

Great Houses of the
Hudson River

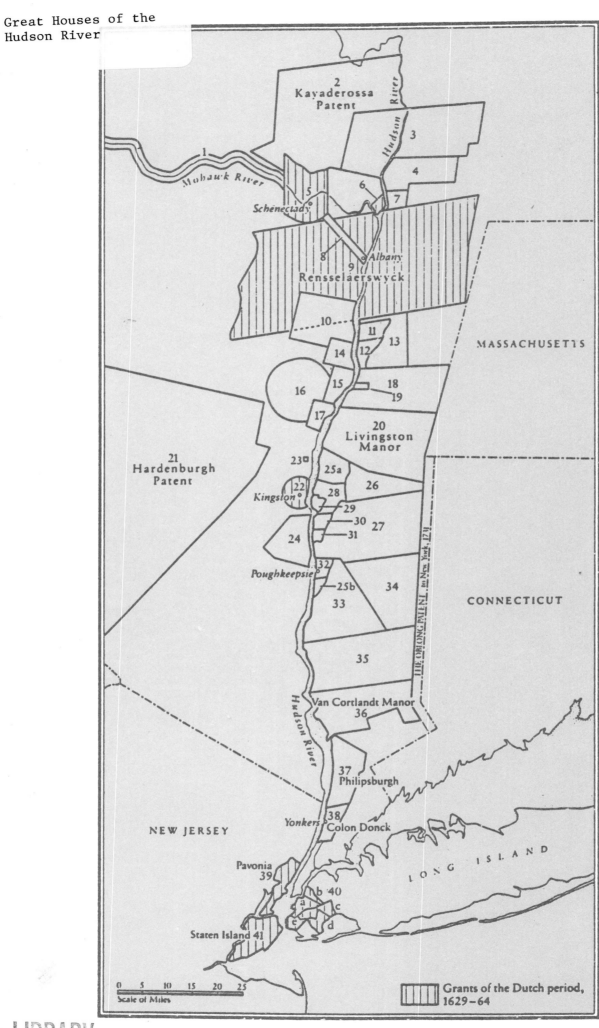

2
Kayaderossa
Patent

Hudson River

3

4

1

Mohawk River

5

6

7

Schenectady

8

9 Albany

Rensselaerswyck

MASSACHUSETTS

10

11

13

14

12

16

15

18

19

17

20
Livingston
Manor

23

25a

21
Hardenburgh
Patent

26

22

28

Kingston

29

30

27

24

31

THE OBLONG PATENT. to New York, 1731

32

Poughkeepsie

25b

34

CONNECTICUT

33

35

Van Cortlandt Manor

36

Hudson River

37
Philipsburgh

Yonkers
38
Colon Donck

NEW JERSEY

LONG ISLAND

Pavonia
39

b 40

a
c

e
d

Staten Island 41

0   5   10   15   20   25
Scale of Miles

Grants of the Dutch period,
1629–64